Ceri Jones &

with Jon Hird

American
Inside Out

Student's Book
A

Advanced

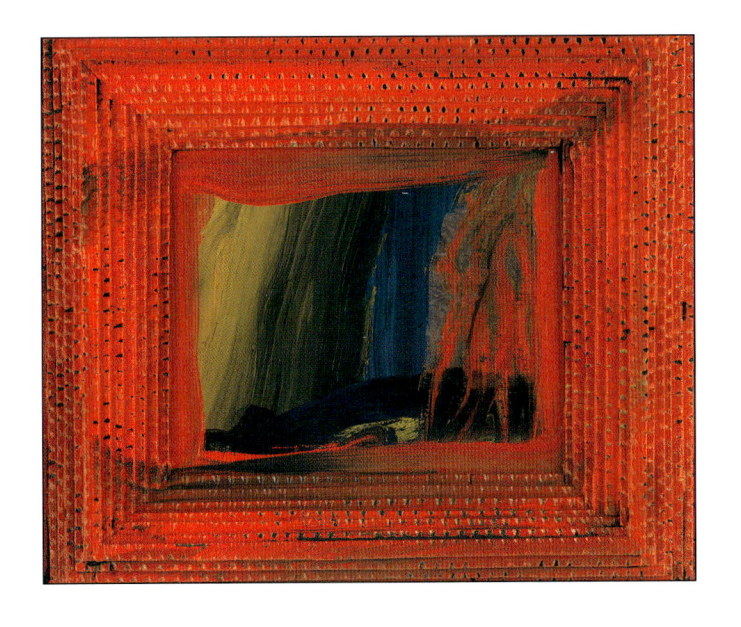

MACMILLAN

Published by Macmillan Education
Between Towns Road, Oxford OX4 3PP
A division of Macmillan Publishers Limited
Companies and representatives throughout the world.
© Macmillan Publishers Limited, 2003

ISBN 978 1 4050 02097 4

Text © Ceri Jones, Tania Bastow, Sue Kay, and Vaughan Jones 2001
Design and illustration © Macmillan Publishers Limited 2001

First published 2001

American Edition 2003

All rights reserved; no part of this publication may be reproduced, stored in a retrieval system, transmitted in any form, or by any means, electronic, mechanical, photocopying, recording, or otherwise, without the prior written permission of the publishers.

Designed by Keith Shaw, Threefold Design
Illustrated by Emma Brownjohn pp. 16, 51, 62; Martina Farrow pp. 15, 43, 46; Julian Mosedale pp. 5, 7, 9, 17, 18, 19, 22, 23, 27, 28, 32, 38, 40, 43, 59, 61; Peter Richardson pp. 11, 48, 52, 53.
Cover design by Andrew Oliver
Cover painting © Howard Hodgkin

Authors' acknowledgments
We would like to thank staff and students at IH Madrid Serrano and the English School of L'Aquila. Special thanks to Bev, Fred, and Rich for their constant support. Also to Fausto Corti, Roberto Giordano, Anna-Maria Ianni, Gianluca Racano, Dafydd Jones, Mandy Grocutt, Melody and Nick Sawyer, and David and Zena Bastow for their help in providing and testing material. A big thank-you also to Karen Warner, our editor, for all her help, hard work, and patience. We are especially grateful to Jon Hird for writing the review units and for his contribution to the Teacher's Book. His comments, along with those of Peter Maggs, were much appreciated. Similarly, our thanks to Russell Stannard (*Inside Out* Workbook), Helena Gomm (*Inside Out* Teacher's Book), and of course everyone involved in the *Inside Out* Resource Pack.

The authors and publishers would like to thank the following for their help in piloting the material and making comments:
Mary Pickett and Ben Darby, International House, London. Tom Bradbury, London School of English, London. Amanda Smith, Kings Street College, London. Angus Savory, Lake School of English, Oxford. Sarah Briscoe, Regent Oxford, Oxford. Alejandro Zarzalejos, EOI Las Rozas. Elisa Jimenez, EOI Fuenlabrada. Rosa Melgar, EOI Valdezarza. Henny Burke, British Language Centre, Madrid. Fiona Miller, International House, Madrid. Angela Tomkinson, British School Cinecitta, Rome. Tobias Jones, Parma University, Parma. Alison Hayman, Liceo Scientifico "G.B.Grassi," Latina. Jennifer Malia and Neil Tibbetts, British Institutes, Milan. Patrick McCann, Linguaviva, Rome. We would also like to thank teachers and staff at the Escuelas Oficial de Idiomas of Spain for their help in the early stages of the project, in particular at A Coruña, Alcala de Guadaira-Seville, Alcorcón, Barcelona 1, Barcelona 2, Bilbao, Cartagena, Ciudad Lineal, Fuenlabrada, Gandía, Getafe, Jesus Maestro-Madrid, Mostoles, Pamplona, San Blas, San Sebastián de los Reyes and Santander.

The publishers wish to thank Steven Poole and Helen East

Excerpts from *Men Are From Mars, Women Are From Venus* by Dr. John Gray (HarperCollins Inc., 1992), © J.G Productions, Inc. 1992, reprinted by permission of HarperCollins Publishers Ltd. **My Girl** Words and Music by Michael Barson © EMI Music Publishing Ltd., London, WC2H 0QY 1979, reprinted by permission of EMI Songs Ltd., London, WC2H 0QY and International Music Publications Ltd. All Rights Reserved. **Excerpts** from *Spain Lonely Planet Guidebook* (Lonely Planet, 1997) and excerpts from www.lonelyplanet.com.au all reprinted by permission of the publisher. **Carol Ann Duffy** "Stealing" from *Selling Manhattan* (Anvil Press Poetry, 1987), reprinted by permission of the publisher. **Excerpt** from *That's Not What I Meant* by Deborah Tannen (Morrow, 1986), © Morrow 1986, reprinted by permission of Time Warner Books UK. **Excerpt** from "After the Jackpot" from *People Weekly* 6/10/02 © Time Inc. 2002, reprinted by permission of People/InStyle Syndication. All Rights Reserved. **Excerpt** from *The Man Who Mistook His Wife for a Hat* by Oliver Sacks (Duckworth, 1985), © Oliver Sacks 1985, reprinted by permission of the Wylie Agency. **I'm Going Slightly Mad** Words and Music by Freddie Mercury, Brian May, Roger Taylor, and John Deacon, © Queen Music Ltd. 1991, reprinted by permission of the Queen Music Ltd./EMI Music Publishing Ltd., London WC2H 0QY, International Music Publications and Watanabe Music Publishing Co. Ltd. for Japanese rights. All rights reserved. **Excerpt** from "Deeply in Love" published in *The Shropshire Star* 7/15/99, reprinted by permission of the publisher. **Excerpt** from "Crisis Point" published in *Birmingham Evening Post* 02/03/00, reprinted by permission of the publisher. **Excerpt** from *Smarties: All the Incredible Facts You Ever Need to Know* by Mike Ashley (Robinson Children's Books, 1999), reprinted by permission of Constable & Robinson Publishing Ltd. **Excerpt** from "Whole in One" published in *Western Daily Press* 3/11/99, reprinted by permission of the publisher.

Although every effort has been made to contact copyright holders before publication, this has not always been possible. If notified, the publisher undertakes to rectify any errors or omissions at the earliest opportunity.

The authors and publishers would like to thank the following for permission to reproduce their photographs:
Aquarius Library p. 4 (b); Anthony Blake Photo Library p. 20; The Bridgewater Book Company Ltd. p. 44 (scarab, peacock feathers, horn, dragon, blue eye); © Barnabas Bosshart/Corbis p.138; © Bettmann/Corbis (a) (d) p. 4; © Rufus F. Folkks/Corbis (c) p. 4; © Dallas and John Heaton/Corbis p. 30; SIN/Corbis p. 11; © John-Marshall Mantel/Corbis p. 13; © Leif Skoogfors/Corbis p. 14; © Kurt Stier/Corbis p. 44; Micheal S. Yamashita/Corbis p. 17 (t); Ronald Grant Cinema Archive/Twentieth Century Fox p. 50; Image Bank pp. 10, 17 (b), 24, 36, 42; Images Colour Library p. 34 (l); Military Photo Library p. 14 (2); © The Museum of Modern Art, New York p. 33 (Hopper, Edward); © Nova Development Corporation and its licensors pp. 45; Ronald Toms/www.osf.co.uk p. 63 (b); *People Weekly* © 2002 Time Inc. All Rights Reserved p. 44; Pictor pp. 31, 65; Powerstock/Zefa pp. 14 (3); Simon Fowler/© Queen Productions Ltd. p. 62; Rex Features pp. 63 (t); Mehau Kulyk/Science Photo Library pp. 54 (scan); Stone pp. 14 (1, 4), 26, 30, 34 (r), 39, 47, 59, 66; Telegraph Colour Library p. 34 (m)

Commissioned photographs by Gareth Boden pp. 13, 14 (food), Haddon Davies p. 55

Cartoons on pp. 11, 49 reproduced with permission of Punch Limited; pp. 21, 29, 35 reproduced with permission of Private Eye.

Printed and bound in Thailand.

2012 2011 2010 2009 2008
12   11   10   9   8   7

Units and topics	Speaking and writing	Reading and listening texts	Grammar, Vocabulary, and Pronunciation
1 Identity What makes you *you* The gender gap Relationships Mistaken identity page 4	Recognizing famous people Discussing what gives you your identity Discussing an ambiguous situation and photographs A phone conversation **Anecdote:** talking about your job, hometown, or family Writing about another student in the class	People describing what gives them their identity Excerpts from *Men Are From Mars, Women Are From Venus*, by John Gray Song: *My Girl*, by Madness Boyfriend and girlfriend arguing on the phone A case of mistaken identity	**G** Adverbials: types and position Phrasal verbs with objects **L** Vocabulary of personal values Word building **P** Getting angry
2 Taste Food Restaurant reviews Good taste page 14	If you were a food… Talking about food associations Discussing good taste **Game:** expanding sentences **Anecdote:** describing your favorite restaurant Writing a restaurant review	People talking about the food they associate with certain situations People describing food experiences abroad Article: a restaurant review Friends discussing good taste	**G** Describing nouns Order of adjectives Test yourself: past tenses Reverse word order **L** Combinations with *taste* **P** Expressing enthusiasm and reservations Expressions for agreeing and disagreeing
3 City Cities of the world Danger in the city Boredom page 24	World city quiz Talking about towns and cities Discussing the dangers of cities Talking about boredom **Anecdote:** describing a city that made an impression on you Writing a short newspaper story Writing a description of a famous town or city	A radio show Friends discussing a newspaper article Excerpts from travel guides Information about Times Square Friends discussing the dangers of living in the city Poem: *Stealing*, by Carol Ann Duffy	**G** Hedging Negative and limiting adverbials **L** City combinations Informal vocabulary **P** Adding emphasis: *just, really, actually*
4 Talk Conversations Tendencies and habits Jokes and funny stories page 34	Finding someone who… Talking about conversations Telling jokes and funny stories **Anecdote:** talking about a member of your family	People talking about what makes a good conversation Excerpt from *That's Not What I Meant*, by Deborah Tannen Eavesdropping on conversations Someone talking about family members, their habits, and their characteristics	**G** Test yourself: *wh-* words General tendencies Past tendencies **L** Expressions with *conversation* Vocabulary of talking and conversations Expressions with *talk* **P** Telling a funny story
5 Luck The lottery Wishes and regrets A sci-fi story page 44	Talking about luck **Anecdote:** an event that has influenced your life **Game:** Wishful Thinking Writing the diary of a survivor of the invasion of the Triffids	Friends discussing good-luck charms Article: *Winning the Big One*—a lottery winner's story Friends discussing the reading text Someone telling the story of a theft Excerpts from *The Day of the Triffids*, by John Wyndham	**G** Unreal conditionals Wishes and regrets **L** Cultural items Descriptive verbs *Wish*
6 Mind A medical case Senses Pet psychology page 54	Finding out what you know about the brain Discussing the five senses Discussing pets	Excerpt from *The Man Who Mistook His Wife for a Hat*, by Dr. Oliver Sacks People discussing the senses A case of pet psychology Song: *I'm Going Slightly Mad*, by Queen	**G** Verbs of the senses Participial clauses **L** Verbs about seeing *Mind* and its expressions **P** Word linking
7 Review 1 page 63			

• *Additional material* page A68 • *Verb structures* page A74 • *Grammar glossary* & *Phonetic symbols* page A76 • *Tapescripts* page A77

1 Identity

1 Do you recognize these famous people?

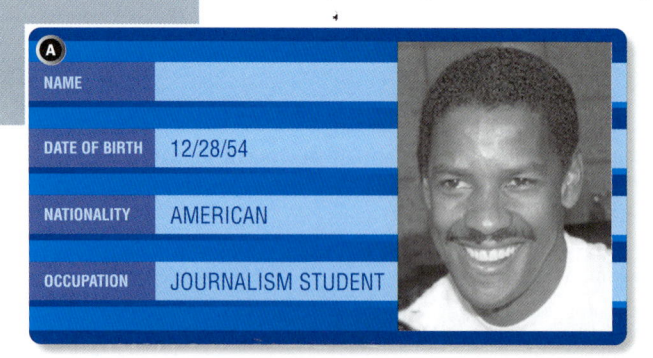

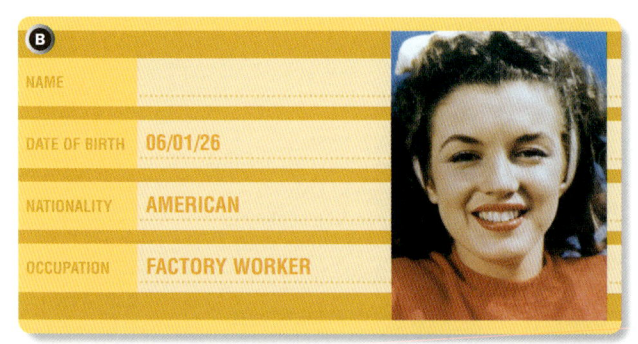

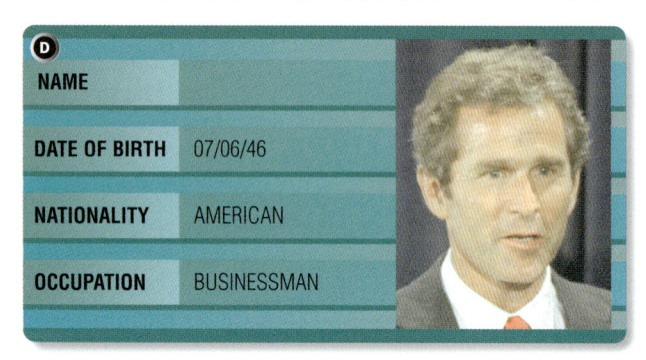

A
NAME
DATE OF BIRTH 12/28/54
NATIONALITY AMERICAN
OCCUPATION JOURNALISM STUDENT

B
NAME
DATE OF BIRTH 06/01/26
NATIONALITY AMERICAN
OCCUPATION FACTORY WORKER

C
NAME
DATE OF BIRTH 04/28/74
NATIONALITY SPANISH
OCCUPATION MODEL

D
NAME
DATE OF BIRTH 07/06/46
NATIONALITY AMERICAN
OCCUPATION BUSINESSMAN

2 Check your answers on page A68.

3 Work with a partner and discuss these questions:
   a) What documents do you usually use to identify yourself?
   b) Do you always carry ID? Is this required by law in your country?
   c) When are you usually asked to show your ID?
   d) What information does your ID give about you?
   e) Do you have any ID on you right now?
   f) Do you like the picture? When was it taken?

Born and Bred

1 Work in small groups and answer these questions:
   a) Where is your hometown? Were you born there? If yes, were your parents born there too?
   b) When someone asks you where you're from, what do you say? If that person was a foreigner and obviously didn't know your country very well, would your answer be the same?
   c) Which is most important to you in defining who you are: your hometown, your country, your language, your job, or something else? Why?

2 01 Listen to Steve, David and Valeria answering some of the questions above. Take short notes on their answers. Which questions did they answer?

3 Compare answers with a partner and discuss these questions:
   a) Which person in 2 do you identify most closely with? Why?
   b) Were any of their answers similar to the ones your group gave in 1?

Close-up

Types of adverbials

Language Reference p. 6

1 Look at the sentences below. Underline all the *adverbials*.

   a) I always stress the fact that I'm Canadian and not American.
   b) I live in northern New Jersey.
   c) I've lived there since I left home.
   d) I went there to study medicine.
   e) I really like living there.

2 Work with a partner and look at these six lines from the recording. Two or three adverbials have been removed from each. Put the adverbials in the correct places in the sentences. They are given in the order you hear them.

For example:
… that's a hard one, because I've traveled around ⁄ a lot ⁄. I guess, uh, Miami. I mean, I lived there ⁄ for more than twenty years ⁄, and that's where I was born.
a lot / for more than twenty years

   a) He's become an American citizen, and he's proud of that…
      just / after thirty-five years of living there / really

   b) …people just assume that I'm American, or maybe they're using the word *American* to mean *North American*.
      sometimes / when I'm traveling / just

   c) I guess it's possible to stick to one language.
      just / in other parts of Canada

   d) …I've lived here, and so has my family. My family has lived in the same house.
      all my life / actually / for five generations

   e) …I like the idea that I'm the fourth generation of doctors in the family and that a woman can carry on what was a male family tradition.
      really / basically / until very recently

3 🔊 02 Listen again and check your answers.

4 Look at the adverbials that were removed in 2. Put them into the categories below.

   a) describes how often something happens
   b) intensifies an adjective
   c) emphasizes the verb
   d) describes where the action happens
   e) describes when the action happens
   f) indicates how long an action continued for
   g) comments on the noun phrase

Position of adverbials

Language Reference p. 6

1 Work with a partner. Look at the sentences below. Where would you normally place the adverb *always* in each of them?

   • We define ourselves according to our place of birth.
   • We have defined ourselves according to our place of birth.
   • We would have defined ourselves according to our place of birth.
   • We wouldn't have defined ourselves according to our place of birth.

Identity UNIT 1

2 Look at this sentence again and answer the questions.

$^{(1)}$ We $^{(2)}$ define $^{(3)}$ ourselves $^{(4)}$ according to our place of birth $^{(5)}$.

a) In which position, 1–5, would you normally add each of these adverbials to this sentence?
- when we are children
- if we live there
- on the whole
- often
- to some extent
- probably

b) Which adverbials would you not use in position 2?

c) In which position can you never add an adverbial?

3 Modify the model sentence in 2 to fit your own opinion as closely as possible.

4 Look at these pairs of sentences. The adverbials in *italics* are in different positions. How does this change the meaning of the sentence?

For example:
A *Actually*, he's performing in the play tomorrow. (and not doing something else)
B He's *actually* performing in the play tomorrow. (and not just sitting in the audience)

1A *Only* Kate knows how to look after horses.
1B Kate *only* knows how to look after horses.

2A *Honestly*, I can't speak to her anymore.
2B I can't speak to her *honestly* anymore.

3A *Earlier*, I had wanted Rich to come to the meeting.
3B I had wanted Rich to come to the meeting *earlier*.

5 Interview another student and write a profile of him/her for a class magazine. Use at least five adverbials.

Language Reference: Adverbials

An adverbial can be a word (*usually, really, probably, softly*) or a phrase (*at home, once a week, to get a good job, when I was a child*). We generally use an adverbial to provide additional information about a verb or an adjective.

Types of adverbials

Adverbials fulfill a number of functions.

1   We can use them to add information about the verb by
   a) describing how often something happens
      *I speak to my mother on the phone **every other day**.*
   b) describing where the action happens
      *I was mugged **on the way home**.*
   c) describing when the action happens
      *The dinner will probably be ready **by then**.*
   d) telling us how long an action continued for
      *He'd been dreaming about it **for months**.*

2   We can use them to give extra information about adjectives; for example, by grading them.
    *He was **extremely** happy to see her.*
    *It was **fairly** hot for the time of year.*

3   We can use them to comment on a clause or focus attention on one part of it.
    ***Generally speaking**, the trains are very quick and efficient.*
    ***Frankly**, I didn't believe a word they said.*
    *I've **actually** lived here for five years now.*

Position of adverbials

We can use adverbials in three positions in a sentence.

1   Initial position
    On the whole, *I prefer to eat homemade food.*

2   We generally use one-word adverbials of frequency, emphasis, and probability in the mid position.
   a) between the subject and the main verb
      *I **never** trusted him.*
   b) between an auxiliary and the main verb
      *I've **always** loved traveling by train.*
   c) In negative sentences the adverb can be placed either between the subject and a negative auxiliary
      *I **really** don't think you should be doing that.*
      or directly after the negative auxiliary
      *I don't **really** think you should be doing that.*
      Adverbs of probability usually follow the first pattern, and adverbs of frequency usually follow the second:
      *They **probably** didn't mean to offend you.*
      *I don't **always** get along with him.*

3   We generally use longer adverbial phrases and adverbs of manner in the final position.
    *They finished the job **as quickly as they could**.*

Changing the position of the adverb can change the meaning of the sentence:

Only *Sarah has Pierre's e-mail address.* (no one else has it)
*Sarah has **only** Pierre's e-mail address.* (and nobody else's)

UNIT 1 *Identity*

I Am Who I Am

Anecdote

LANGUAGE TOOLBOX

Stressing importance

I guess it really means a lot to me…
It's really an important part of my life…
It's kind of central to who I am, I guess…

Running out of things to say

Let me see…
I think that's it.
There's really not much else to say.
I'm not sure what else I can tell you.
Do you know what I mean?

1 Which do you identify most strongly with: your job, your hometown, or your family? You are going to describe the importance of one of these three things to a partner. Choose which one you are going to describe and read the questions below. Think about what you are going to say and the language you will use.

Your job

- [ ] What do you do?
- [ ] How long have you done it for?
- [ ] Did you need to study a lot to do it?
- [ ] Have you always wanted to do this job?
- [ ] Does anybody else in your family do the same job?
- [ ] What do you enjoy most about your job?
- [ ] Is there anything you don't enjoy?
- [ ] Do you think you will continue in the same job for the rest of your working life?
- [ ] Is there anything else you'd like to add?

Your hometown

- [ ] Do you still live there? If yes, do you think you will ever leave? If not, would you like to go back there to live sometime?
- [ ] How long have you lived there/did you live there?
- [ ] Has your family lived there for generations, or do your parents come from somewhere else?
- [ ] What's your favorite place in the town? Why?
- [ ] At what time of year is the town at its best? And its worst?
- [ ] Is it famous for anything? Do tourists come to visit it?
- [ ] Is there anything else you'd like to add?

Your family

- [ ] Do you come from a big family?
- [ ] How many brothers and sisters do you have?
- [ ] Do you have any children?
- [ ] Who do you get along with best of all?
- [ ] Is there anyone in your family you don't get along with?
- [ ] Are you a close-knit family?
- [ ] What kind of things do you do together?
- [ ] How much time do you spend together?
- [ ] Do you prefer spending time with your family or with your friends?
- [ ] Do you go on vacation with your family?
- [ ] Is there anything else you'd like to add?

2 Work with a partner. Tell him/her about the thing you identify most strongly with.
As you listen to your partner's anecdote, make a note of any questions you'd like to ask.
When your partner has finished, ask your questions.

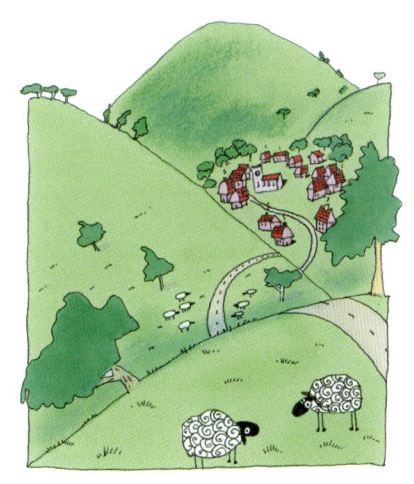

Identity **UNIT 1**

The Gender Gap

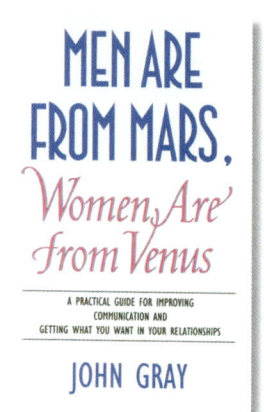

1 Work in small groups and discuss these questions. Which question generates the most discussion?

a) If you were a member of the opposite sex, how would your life be different?
b) To what extent does our society expect men and women to fulfill different roles?
c) Do you think men and women think differently or perceive the world differently?

2 You are going to read an excerpt from a book that explores the differences between men and women. Work with a partner. Read this blurb from the book jacket and answer the questions that follow.

> Once upon a time Martians and Venusians met, fell in love, and had happy relationships together because they respected and accepted their differences. Then they came to Earth and amnesia set in: they forgot they were from different planets.
>
> Using this metaphor to illustrate the commonly occurring conflicts between men and women, Dr John Gray explains how these differences can come between the sexes and prohibit mutually fulfilling loving relationships. Based on years of successful counselling of couples and individuals, he gives advice on how to counteract these differences in communication styles, emotional needs, and modes of behaviour to promote a greater understanding between individual partners.

(Excerpt from *Men Are From Mars, Women Are From Venus*, by John Gray, Ph.D.)

a) Have you read the book? If you have, did you enjoy it? If you haven't read it, have you heard of it? What kind of book is it? Who was it written for? What do you think the main idea is?
b) The book is based on the premise that men and women are very different. The author mentions three categories of differences: communication styles, emotional needs and modes of behavior. What do you think the differences are?
c) Which of the following do you think the author associates with men and which with women?

> uniforms   self-help books   romance   sports   clothes   power
> gadgets and gizmos   spirituality   communication   shopping

3 Work with a partner. You are each going to read an excerpt where the author highlights the main differences between the two sexes.

Student A: Read about life on Mars on page A68.
Student B: Read about life on Venus on page A70.

4 Use your notes to tell your partner about your excerpt and then discuss these questions:

a) Do you identify with the description given of your sex?
b) Are men and women really different?

Vocabulary

1 Does each of these sentences refer to men or women?

a) ____ value power, efficiency, and achievement.
b) The issue of competence is very important to ____ .
c) ____ value love, communication, beauty, and relationships.
d) ____ experience fulfillment through sharing and relating.
e) ____ feel satisfaction when they win a race, achieve a goal, or solve a problem.
f) ____ take pride in being considerate of the needs and feelings of others.
g) ____ are always doing things to prove themselves and develop their power and skills.

2 Find words or phrases in the sentences in 1 to match the definitions below.

a) the knowledge and abilities that enable you to do something well, which can often be learned
b) something that someone has succeeded in doing, especially after a lot of effort
c) the general ability to do something well or efficiently
d) the quality of being able to do a task successfully without wasting time or effort
e) the pleasure you feel when you have done something well
f) the feeling you have when a hope, dream, or ambition has been realized
g) thoughtful toward other people
h) to think that something is important and to appreciate it

3 Create a chart and complete it with the verb, noun, adjective, and adverb forms for your answers to 2 where appropriate.

For example:

noun	verb	adjective	adverb
skills	–	skillful / skilled	skillfully

4 Complete these sentences using words from 3.

a) I always try to take other people's points of view into ____ before making a decision.
b) I find helping others very ____ .
c) Honesty is the thing I ____ most in a friend.
d) I always feel really ____ when I manage to make a deadline.
e) Graduating has been my greatest ____ so far.
f) I really admire people who are very ____ and always manage to do everything on time.
g) My job is the one thing that gives me real ____ .
h) Using a computer is probably one of the most important ____ I've learned in my present job.
i) Feeling ____ about doing my job gives me confidence.

5 Do you agree with the sentences in 4? If not, change them so they are true for you.

6 Work with a partner and compare answers.

Identity UNIT 1 9

Close-up

Phrasal verbs with objects

1 🔊 03 Listen to Martha and Liz discussing the book *Men Are From Mars, Women Are From Venus* and answer the following questions:

a) Have they both read the whole book?
b) What do they think of it?
c) Which passages from the book do they discuss?

2 Work with a partner. Look at the statements below. Are they true or false according to the conversation you've just heard?

a) Neither of them has read the book; they've only had a chance *to look at* it *very quickly and superficially*.
b) Both think the Mars/Venus metaphor is a good way *to communicate* the idea of the difference between the sexes.
c) The book claims that men prefer *to find solutions to* their problems by talking to someone.
d) The book suggests that men tend *to reflect on* their problems.
e) The book suggests that women tend *not to show* their feelings.
f) The book suggests that women do not like *to discuss* their problems.
g) The book suggests that men's refusal to talk about their problems tends *to depress* women.
h) The main solution the author is able *to propose* is to learn to understand and *to tolerate* our differences.

Martha and Liz

3 Listen again and check your answers.

4 Look at the sentences in 2 again. Match the phrases in *italics* to the phrasal verbs below.

1 to figure out   4 to flip through   7 to talk over
2 to bottle up   5 to think through   8 to get across
3 to put up with   6 to get down   9 to come up with

5 Work with a partner. Look at the three types of phrasal verbs that are followed by objects shown below and answer the questions.

Type 1
Two of the sentences below are not correct. Which are they?
a) She flipped the book through.   c) She flipped it through.
b) She flipped through the book.   d) She flipped through it.

(Language Reference p. 12)

Type 2
One of the sentences below is not correct. Which is it?
a) The metaphor gets the idea across well.   c) The metaphor gets it across well.
b) The metaphor gets across the idea well.   d) The metaphor gets across it well.

Type 3
What is the correct word order for these sentences?
a) differences we others' put should each with to learn up.
b) author with what up solution did the come?

6 Answer these questions:

a) What are the rules for word order in types 1 and 2?
b) Are type 3 verbs similar to type 1 or type 2?

7 Look at the other phrasal verbs in 4. Are they type 1, 2, or 3?

UNIT 1 *Identity*

I can't stand him, but I really like dressing him up.

8 Complete each sentence below with a phrasal verb from 4. Put the object (in parentheses) in the right position.

  a) I try not to ____ ; it's always much better to talk about them with a friend. (my feelings)
  b) I hate asking people for help. I'd much rather ____ by myself. (my problems)
  c) I don't often buy a newspaper, but sometimes I ____ at the coffee shop. (one)
  d) I'm not a very confident speaker. Sometimes I'm not sure I ____ very effectively. (my ideas)
  e) My motto is "If you can't change it, then you'll just have to ____ ." (it)
  f) I have a tendency to be too impulsive and don't ____ enough. (things)
  g) I hate arguments; I'd much rather ____ quietly and calmly. (things)
  h) My sister's a really happy, positive person; nothing ever ____ . (her)

9 Are the sentences in 8 true for you? If not, change them so that they are true. Compare answers with a partner.

My Girl

1 Work with a partner. Make a list of five common complaints girlfriends and boyfriends make about each other. Do the complaints differ according to their sex?

2 You're going to listen to a song about an argument between a couple. Look at these expressions from the song. What do you think the problem between them is?

had enough	on my own	why can't I explain
we argued just the other night		on the telephone
see the film tonight	lovely to me	I don't care
doesn't understand	talked it over	mad at me

3 04 Listen to the song and put the expressions in the order you hear them.

4 Were your predictions correct? What is the boy complaining about? What is the girl upset about?

Madness

Madness is a popular British band that reached its peak in the 1980s. The group had many hits, including *House of Fun, Baggy Trousers,* and *It Must Be Love.*

Identity **UNIT 1** 11

5 Work with a partner. Role-play the telephone conversation.

Student A: Look at page A69.
Student B: Look at page A71.

6 05 Listen to the conversation. Was it very different from yours?

7 Work with your partner. Here are some lines from the telephone conversation. Do you remember who said each line, the boy or the girl?

a) …pretty stressed out, had a hard day at work, you know, the usual.
b) So, what about the movie?
c) …do you mind if we go another night?
d) What's wrong?
e) I just don't feel like it tonight…
f) Have I done something wrong?
g) But not tonight, right? The football game's more interesting…
h) Should I come and pick you up?
i) Let's just drop it.
j) Whatever. Suit yourself.

8 Listen again and check your answers.

9 What do you think the boy should do now?

Getting angry

1 Work with a partner. Look at these lines from the telephone conversation and discuss the questions that follow.

A But not tonight, right? The football game's more interesting, I guess.
B No, forget it! I wouldn't want you to go out of your way or anything!

a) Does the girl mean what she says?
b) How does she convey her anger?

2 06 Listen to the lines spoken, first in a normal tone and then angrily. What is the difference?

3 Look at tapescript 05 on page A78. Find other phrases where the girl uses an angry tone of voice. Work with a partner and read the conversation aloud.

Language Reference: Phrasal verbs with objects

There are three basic types of phrasal verbs that are used with an object.

Type 1: not separable

verb + particle + object
They **flipped through** the newspaper.
The research group **looked into** it pretty thoroughly.

Type 2: separable

1 verb + object + particle
We **picked** the rest of the group **up** at the corner.
He'll be **bringing** the issue **up** at the next meeting.

2 verb + particle + object
We **brought up** the subject of Harry's birthday party.
John and Linda **broke off** their engagement.

If the object is a pronoun, only the first order is possible: verb + object pronoun + particle
I'm trying to figure it out. ✓
I'm trying to figure out it. ✗

It is better to use the second order if the noun phrase is particularly long:
He **bottled up** all his negative feelings against his mother-in-law until he couldn't stand it any longer.

Note: Distinguishing between type 1 and type 2 isn't easy, but a good dictionary will tell you which pattern any verb follows.

Type 3: two particles

verb + particle + particle + object
In this type of phrasal verb, the particles are not separable.
I had to **come up with** a solution quickly.
I've always **looked up to** my father.

Mistaken Identity

1. Work with a partner. Read this passage and decide whether each statement that follows is true, false or unknown.

> A young man drove a car into a parking lot. He had just thought how poorly lit it was when a man appeared next to the car and said, "Give me the keys." The owner of the car reluctantly handed over a large bunch of keys. The car was driven away at high speed. A little later, a police officer arrived.

   a) The car was driven into the parking lot.
   b) The young man parked the car.
   c) A man demanded the car keys.
   d) The driver handed over the keys.
   e) The car was stolen.
   f) The police were called shortly after the incident.
   g) A policewoman arrived.
   h) Three people are involved in the story.

2. Check your answers on page A72.

3. The text is *not* describing a car robbery. What do you think the situation might be? Work with your partner and think of a story that makes sense with all the facts given in the passage.

4. Tell your story to the class. Whose story was the most original?

5. Work with a partner. Look at the three pictures below. What do you think is happening in each one?

6. Turn to page A68 and read about the three situations. Were you right?

7. Have you ever interpreted a situation incorrectly or jumped to the wrong conclusions? Discuss your answer with a partner.

Identity UNIT 1

2 Taste

1 Four people were asked, "If you were a food, what food would you be?" Which of the four do you think gave each of the answers below? Why?

| 1 Melody, an art teacher and mother | 2 Nicholas, a U.S. Army officer | 3 David, a sailor | 4 Rita, a retiree |

a) b) c) d)

a) "Baked beans, because they're full of protein and good for you."
b) "A cauliflower, because it's flowery and intricate."
c) "A bar of dark chocolate, because it's smooth and velvety like me!"
d) "Nuts, because they're hard but worth opening for what's inside!"

2 Check your answers on page A68.

3 If you were a food, what would you be? Why? Discuss your answer with a partner.

4 Were there any foods you particularly loved or hated as a child? Do you still love/hate them?

Food Associations

1 What kind of food or drink would you associate with each of the following situations? Why?

a) being in love
b) waiting at an airport
c) rainy days
d) summer
e) the end of a hard day
f) your grandmother's house

2 Work with a partner and discuss your answers. Are your partner's associations very different from yours?

3 07 Listen to six people giving their answers to 1. Answer these questions for each person:

a) Which situation are they talking about?
b) What food do they associate with that situation?

14 UNIT 2 *Taste*

Close-up

Describing nouns

1 How were the foods described by the speakers? Complete the *noun phrases*.

a) b____ coffee i____ a p____ c____
b) a big bowl of f____ salad w____ h____ d____
c) huge slices of r____ beef s____ w____ m____ p____
d) the b____ gravy y____ h____ e____ t____
e) c____ c____-c____ cookies d____ i____ m____
f) s____ r____ strawberries w____ f____ whipped c____
g) some kind of m____ convenience food t____ i____ e____ t____ m____

2 Listen again and check your answers.

3 Work with a partner. Look at the descriptions below. They are all noun phrases with the same subject. What is it?

1 bitter vending-machine coffee in a plastic cup
2 the espresso coffee that you can get in the coffee shop around the corner
3 a cup of strong, black coffee with two or three spoonfuls of sugar
4 fresh-brewed coffee percolated slowly
5 hot coffee with milk steaming in a mug
6 some iced coffee in a tall glass

a) Which description best describes the last cup of coffee you drank?
b) How many different adjectives are used to describe *coffee*?
c) Find a noun that is used to modify *coffee*.
d) Which descriptions follow the pattern *coffee* + preposition + noun phrase?
e) Which descriptions contain a determiner to modify *coffee*?
f) Which descriptions include relative clauses? Which relative clauses are incomplete? Which words have been omitted?

Language Reference p. 16

4 Find an example of each of these structures in the noun phrases in 1.

a) nouns that modify other nouns
b) preposition + noun phrase
c) adjectives
d) complete relative clauses
e) incomplete relative clauses
f) determiners

Which structures go before the noun? Which structures go after it?

5 Complete these descriptions with the words and phrases provided.

a) ____ ____ ____ fruit
   mouthwatering / caramelized / a selection of

b) ____ ____ ____ ____ cake
   chocolate / a / seven-layer / tempting

c) ____ ____ ____ apple pie ____
   just like your grandmother used to make / a helping of / homemade / delicious

d) ____ ____ ____ fish ____ ____
   a white wine sauce / fresh / served in / a dish of / tasty

e) ____ ____ ____ tortilla ____ ____ ____ ____
   spicy / stuffed with / stir-fried / delicious / exquisite / an / vegetables

6 Compare your answers with a partner. Which would you most like to eat?

Taste UNIT 2 15

Order of adjectives

1 Work with a partner. Look at the adjectives in the box and answer the questions that follow.

> mouthwatering   caramelized   spicy   delicious   exquisite   homemade
> tasty   fabulous   tempting

a) Which adjectives express an opinion?
b) Which express a fact?
c) Look at the order of the adjectives in 5 on page 15. Do the "opinion" or the "fact" adjectives come first?

2 What is your favorite dish? Write a complex noun phrase describing it. Read it, in the wrong order, to your partner. Ask your partner to read it back in the right order.

A Game

Round one

1 Look at this simple sentence. Identify the two noun phrases.

The girl was eating an apple.

2 Work in teams. Each team takes turns expanding the sentence by adding more information to the noun phrases. Each team gets a point for each correct modification. The game ends when no further modifications can be made or the sentence is in danger of becoming unintelligible.

Round two

Here is another sentence. Continue to work in teams. Expand the sentence as much as possible in three minutes. The team with the longest and most coherent sentence wins.

The student asked a question.

Language Reference: Describing nouns

The noun phrase

Noun phrases can include

- nouns: *coffee*
- determiners (e.g., *a cup of, some, three, this*): *a cup of coffee*
- adjectives*: *a cup of black coffee*
- descriptive details: *a cup of black coffee with sugar*

*In English, many nouns can function as adjectives.
a **fish** restaurant   **apple** pie

Nouns and adjectives usually come before the nouns they describe. Longer phrases giving more descriptive detail usually go after the noun.

Descriptive details

The description after the noun can be either

- a prepositional phrase (preposition + noun phrase):
  the restaurant **around the corner**
- a relative clause:
  the restaurant **that your cousin recommended**
- a past participle clause:
  the restaurant **recommended by the dining guide**
- or a present participle clause:
  the restaurant **advertising for staff**

Order of adjectives

Adjectives expressing an opinion usually come before adjectives (or nouns) that express a fact.
that **wonderful new** restaurant
that **awful fast-food** place

---

16   UNIT 2   *Taste*

A Taste for Travel

1. ▪▪ 08 Listen to Anne, Kim, Bill, and Steve talking about their eating experiences abroad. Did they like the food in the countries they visited?

2. Listen again and list the food vocabulary you hear each person use.

3. Compare your list with a partner. Which countries do you think they are talking about? Check your answers on page A72.

4. Work with a partner and discuss these questions:

    a) Have you ever eaten food from these countries?
    b) If you have, do you agree with the speakers' opinions? If you haven't, would you like to try it? Why/Why not?

Anne, Kim, Bill, and Steve

Expressing enthusiasm and reservations

1. Look at these excerpts from the recording. Which words do the speakers stress to express their enthusiasm or reservations?

    a) Mmm, it's delicious, really hot and spicy…
    b) Well, it took some getting used to.
    c) Well, to tell you the truth, I didn't really like it that much.
    d) …and, mmm, I don't really like cabbage that much…
    e) …no, it isn't really my favorite.
    f) It isn't particularly elaborate, but it's good.

2. ▪▪ 09 Listen and check your answers.

3. Work with a partner. Look at the two short exchanges below. Use the underlined expressions in 1 and add your own ideas to make the conversations sound a) more enthusiastic b) less enthusiastic.

    A: So how was the trip?
    B: Interesting.

    A: So how was the food last night?
    B: Unusual.

4. Ask your partner about …

    a) the last time he/she ate out.
    b) the last movie he/she saw.
    c) his/her last English class.

    Did he/she enjoy it?

Taste UNIT 2 17

The Demise of a Great Little Restaurant

1 Read the introduction to this restaurant review and answer the questions.

a) When did the writer first visit the restaurant?
b) How is it different from other restaurants? List as many unusual things about it as you can.
c) Why do you think the writer liked it so much?
d) Would you like to eat there?

review

I first reviewed Le Palmier ten years ago. At the time I wrote that it was one of the most unusual and enjoyable seafood restaurants I had ever visited – not least because of its location on Croix St. Michel, a tiny island just off the coast near St. Laurent. Back then it was run by a married couple, Marianne and Didier. He was the cook and fisherman, while she tended the vegetable gardens and ran the restaurant. There was only one waiter, their son Alex.

Access to the island was by a small launch with room for no more than five passengers. You couldn't make reservations. You simply showed up at the jetty in St. Laurent and waited. Eventually Marianne would come along in the launch and pick you up. Sometimes you had to wait for an hour or more. To make the wait more enjoyable, their daughter, Dominique, had set up a tiny bar on the jetty. It was really just a kiosk with a couple of tables where you could have a glass of white wine (from vines grown on the island) and enjoy the scenery.

The trip to the island took ten minutes. As the coastline receded, Marianne would tell you what was on the day's menu and what was going on in the village. She always seemed very well informed. Or, perhaps, very imaginative.

Le Palmier was in the only building on the island: a three-story house looking over the water to the mainland. On the upper floors lived the family. Their rooms had balconies filled with glorious geraniums and bougainvillaea. The restaurant occupied the ground floor, opening out onto a seaside terrace. A striped canopy provided shelter from the sun. There were only four tables, each one covered with a crisp, white linen tablecloth and provided with a basket of wonderful homemade bread.

The menu was, frankly, limited, but while choice was restricted, there were rarely any complaints about price, which was absurdly low, or about quality. Basically, you ate whatever Didier had caught in the waters of the bay that morning. On my first visit, I had squid for the first time in my life. It was barbecued with red peppers and served with fresh salad from the restaurant gardens to the sound of *La Traviata*. Didier was singing in the kitchen. For dessert I chose pears in red wine.

This summer, my wife and I went to St. Laurent as an anniversary celebration, my first visit in several years.

2 Compare your answers with a partner.

3 When the writer went back ten years later, the restaurant had undergone a lot of changes. Work with a partner. Before you read the rest of the review, discuss these questions:

What changes do you think had taken place? Why do you think these changes took place?

4 Work with a partner and read the rest of the review.

Student A: Look at page A71.
Student B: Look at page A73.

5 Discuss these questions with your partner:

a) Would you prefer to eat at Le Palmier as it was or as it is now? Why?
b) What was the writer's attitude toward the changes?
c) Were any of the changes, in your opinion, for the better?
d) Do you know of anywhere that has undergone similar changes?

Vocabulary Work with a partner who read the same text as you and follow the instructions below.

1 Prepare to teach four of these words from your part of the review to a student who read the other part.

   Student A

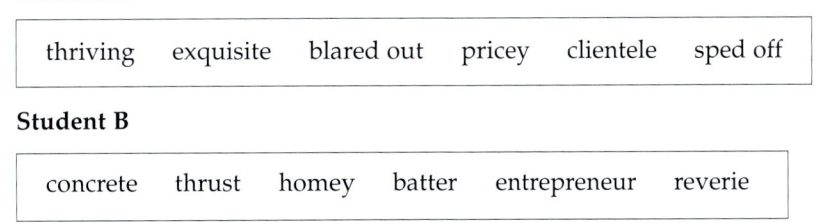

   | thriving | exquisite | blared out | pricey | clientele | sped off |

   Student B

   | concrete | thrust | homey | batter | entrepreneur | reverie |

   a) Read the text again and find the words.
   b) Discuss their meanings with your partner. Think about the best way to explain them.

2 Work with a different partner and teach him/her the words.

3 Ask your partner to write sentences containing the new words.

4 Check that the words have been used correctly in the sentences.

Test Yourself

Past tenses 1 Look at this excerpt taken from the restaurant review. Choose the more appropriate form of each verb.

> Basically, you (1) **ate / were eating** whatever Didier (2) **was catching / had caught** in the waters of the bay that morning. On my first visit, I (3) **had / was having** squid for the first time in my life. It (4) **barbecued / was barbecued** with red peppers and (5) **served / had been served** with fresh salad from the restaurant gardens to the sound of *La Traviata*. Didier (6) **was singing / sang** in the kitchen. (Introduction, lines 40–45)

2 Complete these excerpts with the correct form of each verb in parentheses.

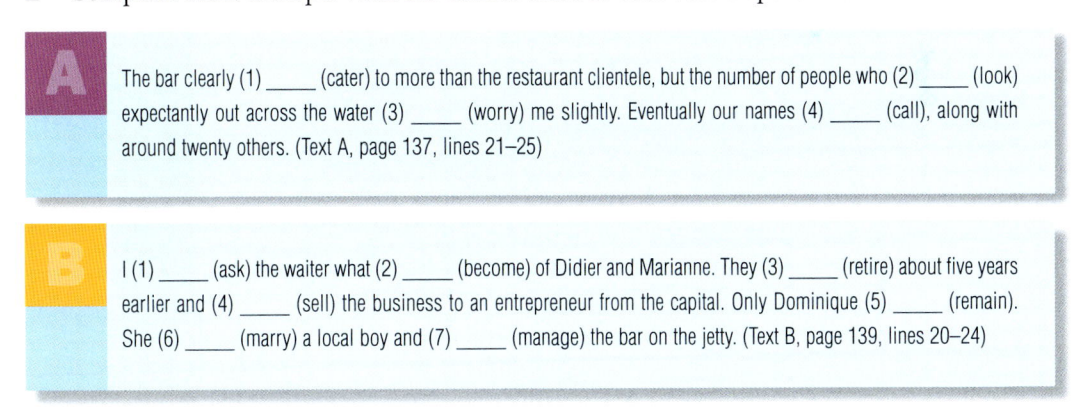

> **A** The bar clearly (1) ____ (cater) to more than the restaurant clientele, but the number of people who (2) ____ (look) expectantly out across the water (3) ____ (worry) me slightly. Eventually our names (4) ____ (call), along with around twenty others. (Text A, page 137, lines 21–25)

> **B** I (1) ____ (ask) the waiter what (2) ____ (become) of Didier and Marianne. They (3) ____ (retire) about five years earlier and (4) ____ (sell) the business to an entrepreneur from the capital. Only Dominique (5) ____ (remain). She (6) ____ (marry) a local boy and (7) ____ (manage) the bar on the jetty. (Text B, page 139, lines 20–24)

3 Check your answers with the review. Discuss with a partner any differences you find.

4 Choose one of the openings below and think about something that has happened to you recently.

   a) I had just gotten in when…
   b) I was walking down the road when…
   c) I was in my car…
   d) It was three o'clock in the morning…
   e) You'll never believe who I saw the other day…
   f) I'd just been…

5 Tell your partner about it.

Taste UNIT 2

Close-up

Reverse word order

1 The sentences below have been taken from the restaurant review. Put the words in the correct order without looking back.

   a) floors family the lived upper on the. (Introduction, line 28)
   b) chat to gone Marianne was with opportunity the. (Text A, line 37)
   c) ran between tables waiters the. (Text B, lines 3–4)

(Language Reference p. 20)

2 Check your sentences with the review and answer these questions:

   a) Are they different?
   b) Why is the word order in the review different from usual?

3 Complete these sentences about a place you remember from your past.

   a) Gone is the…
   b) Many were the…

4 Work with a partner. Compare your sentences and explain the changes that have taken place.

Language Reference: Reverse word order

Reverse word order is when a sentence begins with something other than the subject. We use it to create dramatic effect.

Regular word order

The family lived on the upper floors. →
The days when we could sit back and do nothing are gone. →
The rain came down. →

Reverse word order

On the upper floors lived the family.
Gone are the days when we could sit back and do nothing.
Down came the rain.

Reverse word order is usually used in writing. It is not commonly used in everyday speech.

Food for Thought

Anecdote

1 You are going to tell your partner about one of your favorite restaurants. Decide which restaurant you are going to describe. Think back to the last time you ate there. Look at the questions below and think about what you're going to say and the language you will need.

- ☐ Where is the restaurant?
- ☐ What kind of restaurant is it?
- ☐ When did you last go there?
- ☐ Who did you go with?
- ☐ Was it a special occasion?
- ☐ What did you eat?
- ☐ How often do you go there?
- ☐ Do you always go with the same people?
- ☐ Do you always eat the same thing there?
- ☐ What do you like most about the restaurant?
- ☐ Who first introduced you to it?
- ☐ When do you think you'll go back next?
- ☐ Would you recommend it to your partner?
- ☐ Is there anything else you'd like to add?

2 Tell your partner about the restaurant.

3 Answer these questions:

    a) Which of the following did your partner talk about?
- the food
- the service
- the decor
- the atmosphere
- the company

    b) Which was the most important to your partner?
    c) Which is the most important to you?

Writing

1 Write a review of your favorite restaurant for a local English-language newspaper. Before you start, look at the questions below and think about what you are going to write and the language you will need.

Hmm, it's all so tempting…
Chicken cordon bleu, filet mignon,
perhaps the duck à l'orange…
Oh, what the heck,
I'll have the fish!

    a) Think about what kind of person the restaurant would appeal to and how best to attract this kind of person.
    b) Decide what information you are going to include. Look at the list below:
- the address and phone number
- the opening times
- some information about the people who run the place
- the menu
- some typical dishes
- a description of a particular dish
- a description of the decor
- a description of the atmosphere
- a personal recommendation (a dish; a good time or day to go)
- some information about the history of the place (how long it's been open; the history of the building)
- anything else you'd like to add

2 Decide what order to present the information in.

3 Write your review of about 200 words.

Taste

Combinations

1 How many words can you form from the root word *taste*?

2 Complete these sentences with your answers to 1.

A   He has developed a ____ for expensive champagne.
B   Katherine has marvelous ____ in clothes.
C   The new cafe is very lively, with very ____ food and a good selection of desserts.
D   We found a charming little hotel with ____ furnished bedrooms and lots of facilities.
E   She wore a silk dress in a ____ shade of pink.
F   For years he worked as a tea-____ in China.
G   The beauty of wine-____ is that you learn to appreciate different flavors.
H   This milk ____ as though it's gone bad.
I   You can't beat the ____ of fresh raspberries, straight from the garden.
J   If you have a ____ for fine food, you'll certainly appreciate this new restaurant.
K   It would probably ____ a lot better if it didn't have so much salt in it.
L   The city has something for all ____ , from an impressive museum to a windsurfing lake.
M   The joke was in very poor ____ , and a lot of people were offended.

3 The word *taste* has two basic meanings. What are they?

4 Which of the two meanings do these words and expressions have?

  a) to taste
  b) to be tasty
  c) to be tasteful
  d) to have poor taste
  e) a taste of…

5 Complete these sentences with prepositions.

  a) He has developed a taste ____ French films.
  b) They have incredibly poor taste ____ clothes.

6 Which sentence in 5 talks about choice? Which refers to interest?

7 Choose the correct preposition in each of these expressions:

  a) peculiar taste in/for books
  b) a taste in/for exotic travel
  c) a taste in/for dangerous sports
  d) excellent taste in/for shoes
  e) very good taste in/for music

8 Think of people you know who have these tastes. Tell a partner about them.

A Question of Taste

1 Work with a partner. Write a short definition of *good taste*. Use no more than twenty words.

2 Share your definition with the rest of the class. Which one do you like the best?

3 🔊 10 Listen to Sarah, David, and Angela discussing good taste. Take notes about what they each think good taste is.

4 Compare your notes with a partner. Were your ideas similar to the speakers'?

5 What other quality did they mention? What did the speakers understand this quality to mean?

6 Listen again and check your answers. Do you agree with their definitions of this quality?

Agreeing and disagreeing

1 Look at these excerpts from the discussion. Words are missing from each excerpt. The missing expressions are used to express agreement or disagreement. Decide which type of expression is missing in each blank.

a) Sarah: …I can't believe he bought her plastic flowers for her birthday. I mean, that is so tacky. That is such bad taste.
   Angela: (1) ____ . It's the thought that counts.
   David: (2) ____ ! Plastic flowers don't count!

b) Sarah: Yes, I mean, taste is a very personal thing.
   Angela: Right. Beauty is in the eye of the beholder and that kind of thing.
   Sarah: (3) ____ . Everyone's different so I guess…

c) Angela: …wearing a big gold medallion or something.
   David: (4) ____ ! Things like that are awful, aren't they?
   Angela: Socks!
   David: Socks with sandals, and white socks with black shoes, definitely!
   Sarah: No, (5) ____ ; some people like them.

UNIT 2 *Taste*

d) Sarah: It's knowing what's appropriate that's good taste.
David: (6) _____ . It's also about being able to judge the quality of things. Good quality stuff is usually tasteful. And yes, Sarah, you're right—it's about choosing the right thing at the right time, too.
Angela: That reminds me of Rebecca the other day at Joann's wedding. Talk about the wrong clothes at the wrong time!
Sarah: What, wearing that blue dress thing?
Angela: Yeah, it was obviously expensive, but talk about bad taste.
David: (7) _____ . She looked completely out of place.
Sarah: Well, (8) _____ . But Rebecca, you know, Rebecca has class…

e) Angela: But class is about knowing how to behave, not how to dress.
Sarah: (9) _____ —not these days. Class means being yourself and not caring what other people think.
David: Sure, but I think there's more to it than that. I think it's that you know how to behave in every circumstance, no matter how difficult the situation might be, and how to deal with it. That's class.
Angela: (10) _____ . The feeling that you can take everything in stride…

2 🔊 11 Listen and write down the expressions actually used.

3 What other expressions for agreeing and disagreeing do you know? Do you use similar expressions in your own language?

Intonation

1 🔊 12 Listen to the six times a speaker uses *yes* or *no* in the discussion. Decide whether the speaker

a) is uncertain about what is being said.
b) is in total agreement with what is being said.
c) totally disagrees with what is being said.

2 How does the intonation change according to the meaning the speaker wants to convey?

3 🔊 13 Work with a partner. Listen to six sentences and respond with *yes* or *no* so that your partner can tell if you agree, disagree, or are uncertain.

In Good Taste?

1 Look at this list of actions and decide which of the following you consider:

a) completely unacceptable
b) acceptable in certain circumstances
c) totally acceptable at all times

- chewing gum
- leaving your cell phone on when you're in a restaurant
- kissing in public
- putting your hands in your pockets
- swearing
- losing your temper in public
- asking people how much something they are wearing cost
- eating in the street

2 Compare your views with a partner and answer these questions:

a) Would your parents have given the same answers?
b) Are your answers influenced more by what your parents taught you, what you were taught in school, or what you have experienced in life?

Taste UNIT 2

3 City

1 How much do you know about cities around the world? Take this quiz and find out.

quiz

1 What proportion of the world's population lives in cities?
a) Over 80%   c) About a third
b) About two thirds   d) About half

2 What is the world's largest capital city?
a) Tokyo   c) Mexico City
b) Seoul   d) New Delhi

3 What city has the most automobile traffic in the United States?
a) Los Angeles   c) Miami
b) New York   d) Chicago

4 What is the world's oldest capital city?
a) Baghdad   c) Cairo
b) Damascus   d) Amman

5 What is the world's highest capital city?
a) La Paz (Bolivia)   c) Quito (Ecuador)
b) Lima (Peru)   d) Kathmandu (Nepal)

6 What was the first city to reach a population of 1 million?
a) Mexico City   c) London
b) New York   d) Rome

2 14 Listen and check your answers.

Close-up

Hedging

1 Look at these excerpts from the radio program and complete the sentences.

a) It ____ ____ that there is a steady movement toward urban areas…

b) …there is still some ____ as to what the world's largest capital is.

c) …it is ____ ____ that Los Angeles is the U.S. city that suffers from the worst traffic conditions.

d) It's ____ ____ whether this information is based on popular opinion or on statistical data, however.

e) Sources ____ to suggest that the Syrians are right…

f) There is ____ ____ ____ about which of the world's capital cities is the highest.

(Language Reference p. 25)

2 15 Listen and check your answers.

3 Work with a partner. Which of the statements in 1 does the speaker believe is based on
a) very strong evidence?   c) weak evidence?
b) fairly strong evidence?   d) unreliable evidence?

UNIT 3 City

4 Use the expressions in 1 to write sentences about the following data.

	REPORT 1	REPORT 2
Two new reports have just been published in which people living in cities and suburbs were asked about how happy they are with where they live. Below are some of the results.		
People who enjoy living in cities	79%	72%
People who live in cities but would prefer to live in the suburbs	35%	43%
People who live in cities but spend as much time as possible outside of cities	47%	29%
People who live in suburban areas but would prefer to live in cities	62%	36%
Percentage of these who are under 30	84%	–
Percentage of these who are over 50	13%	–
Number of people in the sample	?	?

5 Which group(s) would you have fallen into? Compare your answer with a partner.

6 Look at these four newspaper headlines. What do you think the story is behind each one? Discuss your ideas with a partner.

A **LIFE HEALTHIER AT HALF A MILE ABOVE SEA LEVEL**

C **SOCCER CAUSES SOCIAL UNREST**

D **SEDENTARY LIFESTYLE CHANGING SHAPE OF OUR BODIES**

B **MANY YOUNG PEOPLE WOULD PREFER TO LIVE IN CITIES**

7 16 Listen to two people discussing one of the stories. Which story are they talking about? Were your ideas about the story right?

8 Listen again and take notes about the facts of the story.

9 Work with a partner. Write the story as you think it would have appeared in the "News in Brief" section of the newspaper. Compare your story to the version on page A69.

Language Reference: Hedging

Sometimes we do not want to state a fact too categorically if we are not sure that we can prove that it is true. We can use a range of expressions to distance ourselves from facts and opinions. This is called *hedging*.

Hedging with verbs

We can use *appear* and *seem (that)* to create a distance between ourselves and what we say.

It **seems that** the president may soon resign.
It **appears that** the news reports are true.
The weather **appears** to be changing.
The outcome **seems** to be inevitable.

To add further distance, we can use the modal *would*.

It **would appear that** you have already made up your minds.
They **would appear** to be hostile.
It **would seem that** you are wrong.
It **would seem that** you are avoiding me.

Hedging with the passive voice

We can use passive forms of the verb to show that an opinion is not necessarily our own.

It **is** widely **recognized** that the future of advertising is on the Net.
It **is believed that** there are no survivors.
It **is not known** whether he will accept the offer.

Hedging with noun phrases

We can use the following noun phrases to hedge around a subject.

There is little doubt that she took her own life.
There is some doubt that the country can control its inflation.
There is no doubt that he knows what he's doing.
There is little evidence of your ability to manage change.

Where in the World?

1 Work with a partner. Discuss the following questions:

a) What is the capital of your country famous for? Does it attract a lot of visitors?
b) Which capital city would you most like to spend a weekend in?
c) Do you live in a city, in the suburbs, or out in the country? Have you always lived there? Do you like it? Why/Why not?

2 The following excerpts from travel guides describe five of the world's most famous cities. Work in small groups. Read the descriptions and decide what city is being described in each text.

1 lonely planet

There is little point in portraying it as something it is not. Its beauty is not as awe-inspiring as other cities. It is not even particularly old, and much of what may have constituted its historical legacy has over the centuries been all too quickly sacrificed to make way for the new. It is a largely modern city, a product of the 19th and 20th centuries, and the expanses of its outer dormitory suburbs and peripheral high-rise apartment jungles are an oppressive introduction for anyone driving into the city for the first time.

It may lack the historical richness and sophistication of other European capitals, but it oozes a life and character that, given the opportunity to work its magic (it doesn't take long), cannot leave you indifferent. Leaving aside the great art museums, the splendor of the main square and the Royal Palace, and the elegance of the city park, the essence of this city is in the life pulsing through its streets. In no other European capital will you find the city center so thronged so late into the night as here, especially if you go out on weekends. Everyone seems to stay out late, as though some unwritten law forbade sleeping before dawn. In this sense, it is a city more to be lived than seen. ●

(Adapted from *Lonely Planet* publications)

2

By its mere existence, the city is an oxymoron, where old and new, night and day, land and sea coexist and make it all seem perfectly natural. It is a contrast of sight and sound, yet the distinct, diverse elements blend together in harmony.

The city has one of the most beautiful ports in the world, and its beaches entice tourists from around the world. Yet, while the coastline is a main attraction of the city, the 33,000-square-yard, meadow-lined leisure area—the site where Don Pedro was proclaimed the country's first emperor—draws people inland. While a visitor might even see an agouti (a harmless, tailless rodent) or a coati (a small, racoon-like mammal roaming free in the park, blending in unobtrusively as if they have just as much a right to enjoy the tourist-focused region as humans do, towering mountains surround the endless, smooth white beaches and lively city streets.

By day, the city bustles with tourists savoring culture—museums, concert halls, churches, theaters, the financial center; and nature—beaches, squares, and parks. Yet at night, this metropolis doesn't sleep. There are theaters, dance halls, nightclubs, world-famous discos—some classy, some tacky—and the activity continues into the wee hours. Transportation too is an example of disparate components combining to work together: a complex, seemingly haphazard system of taxis, buses, a subway and a street car forms a functional, practical transit network for those who choose to forgo transportation by foot or even by bicycle.

But however you choose to get around the city, be sure to take in as much as you can of this intense fusion of the modern and the traditional that appeals to all tastes in the 21st century. ●

3 lonely planet

This is a cosmopolitan mixture of the Third and First worlds, of chauffeurs and beggars, of the establishment, the avowedly working class and the avant-garde. Unlike comparable European cities, much of it looks unplanned and grubby, but that is part of its appeal. Visiting the city is like being let loose on a giant-sized Monopoly board clogged with traffic. Even though you probably won't have a clue where you are, at least the names will look reassuringly familiar. The city is so enormous that visitors will need to make maximum use of the underground train system: unfortunately, this dislocates the city's geography and makes it hard to get your bearings. ●

(Adapted from t*Lonely Planet* publications)

4 lonely planet

The sheer level of energy is the most striking aspect of this capital city. It's true that the larger picture can be somewhat depressing—shoebox housing developments and office blocks traversed by overhead expressways crowded with traffic. But this is the country's success story in action. The average suburb hasn't fallen prey to supermarket culture though: streets are lined with tiny specialty shops and bustling restaurants, most of which stay open late into the night. Close to the soaring office blocks exist pockets of another time—an old wooden house, a kimono shop, a small inn, an old lady in traditional dress sweeping the pavement outside her home with a straw broom. More than anything else, this is a place where the urgent rhythms of consumer culture collide with the quieter moments that linger from older traditions. It's a living city, and you'll never run out of things to explore. ●

(Adapted from *Lonely Planet* publications)

5 lonely planet

They don't come any bigger than this—king of the hill, top of the heap. No other city is arrogant enough to dub itself Capital of the World, and no other city could carry it off. It is a densely packed mass of humanity—seven million people in 309 sq. miles (800 sq. km)—and all this living on top of one another makes the inhabitants a special kind of person. Although it's hard to put a finger on what makes it buzz, it's the city's hyperactive rush that really draws people here.

In a city that is so much a part of the global subconscious, it's pretty hard to pick a few highlights—wherever you go you'll feel like you've been there before. Bookstores, food, theater, shopping, people: it doesn't really matter what you do or where you go, because the city itself is an in-your-face, exhilarating experience. ●

(Adapted from *Lonely Planet* publications)

Turn to page A68 if you need help.

3 Look at the excerpts again and underline the information that helped you decide what city was being described.

4 Work with a partner and discuss these questions:

a) Which description appeals to you most? Why? Choose two or three phrases that you find evocative.
b) Have you been to any of these cities? Do the excerpts reflect your experiences?
c) Do the excerpts make you want to visit any of these cities?

Vocabulary

1 Match the definitions (a–h) to the adjectives (1–8) on the right. Then decide which of the adjectives you would use to describe the noun phrases in the box below.

a) very dirty
b) full of people who are very busy or lively (especially a place)
c) not organized; not arranged according to a plan
d) very tall or high in the sky (especially buildings or trees)
e) so loud, big, or noticeable that you just can't ignore it
f) cheap and poorly made or vulgar
g) giving a feeling of respect and amazement
h) blocked so that nothing can pass through (especially a place)

1 awe-inspiring
2 haphazard
3 tacky
4 grubby
5 clogged
6 bustling
7 soaring
8 in-your-face

> plastic souvenirs   treetops   arteries   beauty   advertising campaigns
> children's hands   unplanned method of work   supermarkets   old sneakers
> skyscrapers   waterways   scenery   action movies   vacation postcards
> beach resorts   collection of people

2 Find the adjectives in the excerpts. What are they describing?

3 Work with a partner. Look at the verbs below. Without looking back at the excerpts, match each one with an appropriate phrase from the list on the right.

a) (excerpt 1, line 7)   to make   a finger on (something)
b) (excerpt 1, line 17)   to work   prey to (something)
c) (excerpt 3, line 15)   to get   on top of one another
d) (excerpt 4, line 10)   to fall   its magic
e) (excerpt 5, line 9)   to live   your bearings
f) (excerpt 5, line 11)   to put   way for the new

4 Check your answers with the excerpts and make sure you understand the meanings of the phrases. Use a dictionary if necessary.

5 Complete these sentences, using the phrases in 3. Make any changes to the phrases that are necessary.

a) No matter how stressed you feel, once you let the beauty of the beach and the warmth of the sun ____ on you, you will begin to wind down and relax.
b) The old town is built on the edge of a cliff overlooking the gorge, using up every bit of spare space. Some houses are even built into the cliff face, and people ____ in a warren of narrow cobbled streets.
c) The medieval clock tower offers a landmark that is visible wherever you are in the town, making it very easy ____ .
d) It is difficult ____ exactly what makes this gray, industrial town such a popular tourist destination.
e) It's very easy ____ the charm of the market; stall holders and people often end up spending much more than they'd expected to.
f) Far too often, historic town centers are carved up and charming old buildings torn down ____ .

6 Can any of the words and phrases in 1 and 3 be used to describe your hometown or a place you know well? Discuss your thoughts with a partner.

Close-up

Negative and limiting adverbials

1 Work with a partner. Look at the adverbial phrases in the box and decide which of them have negative or limiting meanings.

> under no circumstances   quite often   only after a long night   never
> not until he'd finished   seldom   at once   frequently   only then   usually
> only after a long wait   not a word   rarely   even in the summer   on no account

(Language Reference p. 29)

2 Look at these sentences and answer the questions that follow.

1A *In no other European capital* **will you find** the city center so thronged so late into the night.
1B **You won't find** the city center so thronged so late into the night *in any other European capital*.
2A *Not until I actually lived there* **did I understand** just how great the lifestyle is.
2B **I didn't understand** just how great the lifestyle is *until I actually lived there*.

a) Which sentence appears in the excerpt about Madrid on page 26?
b) Look at the *adverbial phrases* in the sentences. Which is the more common position for the adverbial? Why has the adverbial phrase been moved in the A sentences?
c) Would the A sentences or the B sentences be more likely to be spoken?
d) What happens to the word order when the adverbial phrase is placed at the beginning of the sentence?

3 Rewrite each sentence below, starting with the word or words given.

For example:
You will rarely see such a superb example of modern architecture.
Rarely *will you see such a superb example of modern architecture.*

a) I rarely visit a city more than once, but this place is really special.
   Rarely…
b) I had never seen anything so breathtakingly beautiful before.
   Never before…
c) You should not go out alone at night under any circumstances.
   Under no circumstances…
d) You will be able to see and feel the heart of this beautiful old town only by wandering down its narrow side streets.
   Only…
e) You will begin to understand the special charm of this place only after you have spent an evening there.
   Only after you…
f) You can't really understand exactly how beautiful the view is until you climb to the top.
   Not until…

4 Think of a town, city, or village to fit each sentence.

Writing

1 You are going to write a short description of a famous town or city in your country.

a) Choose the town or city you are going to write about.
b) Decide what kind of tourist or visitor you are writing for. (Young backpackers? Families? Culture vultures?)
c) Decide on three or four main points to include in your description.
d) Write a short description (about 200 words) in the style of a travel guide. Include at least one inversion and three of the words and expressions from the vocabulary exercises on page 27. Do NOT include the name of the town or city.

2 When you have finished writing, work in groups of three or four. Read your description to the group. Listen to the descriptions and try to guess which town or city each one is describing. What information helped you get the answer?

Language Reference: Negative and limiting adverbials

Sometimes we can place a negative or limiting adverbial in the front position in a sentence to create emphasis. This effect is most frequently found in writing.

Word order

In this type of sentence, the *subject + auxiliary* word order is inverted.
I have never seen anything quite so breathtaking.
Never **have I** seen anything quite so breathtaking.

The same thing happens with the verb *be*.
It is not only one of the oldest cities on Earth, but also one of the most beautiful.
Not only **is it** one of the oldest cities on Earth, but it is also one of the most beautiful.

In the simple present and simple past, use *do/does* or *did*.
We rarely *visit* that part of town.
Rarely **do we visit** that part of town.

Negative adverbials

Not a + noun
Not a word did she say to anyone.

Not until + verb phrase
Not until I got home did I realize how lucky I'd been.

Not until + noun phrase
Not until the end did I realize how lucky I'd been.

Under no circumstances
Under no circumstances are you to leave before you finish the exercise.

On no account
On no account can they claim to be the best.

Never
Never had I seen such a beautiful sight.

No sooner ... than
No sooner had I arrived **than** the doorbell rang.

Limiting adverbials

Only + by + -ing
Only by bribing the police officer was he able to get away.

Only + conjunction + verb phrase
Only if he promised to help would she tell him where he had left his keys.
Only after they had finished their lunch were they allowed outside to play.
Only when I took the test did I realize how little I knew!

Little
Little did they know that we were following them.

Rarely/seldom
Rarely had I seen such a beautiful sight.

Barely/hardly/scarcely... when
Barely had I arrived **when** the doorbell rang.

Anecdote

LANGUAGE TOOLBOX
It was about three years ago...
The one thing that really struck me was...
It's hard to describe...
It's difficult to put into words...
When you arrive, the first thing you see is...
The first thing I noticed was...

1 You are going to describe a visit to a city that made an impression on you. Decide which city you are going to talk about and then look at the questions below. Decide which are relevant to the city you are going to talk about. Think about what you are going to say and what language you will use.

☐ When did you first visit the city? Have you visited it more than once? If so, when was the last time you were there?
☐ What was your overall impression of the place? Is there any one particular image that sticks in your mind? How would you describe the general atmosphere of the city?
☐ Why did you go there? On vacation? For work? To study? Was it your decision or did you go on a trip with friends or your family?
☐ How long did you stay? Where did you stay? What were the people like? What was the weather like?
☐ What did you do? The usual touristy things? Did you sit and watch the world go by or did you walk for miles and miles?
☐ Would you like to go back? Have you made any plans to go back? Would you recommend it to a friend?
☐ Is there anything else you'd like to mention?

2 Tell your partner about the city. Give as much detail as possible.

3 Have you visited the city your partner described? If yes, were your impressions the same? If not, would you like to visit it after hearing your partner's description? Why/Why not?

This is John Trimp from the town planning department. He's here to demonstrate the proposals for the old town.

One Big Party

1 Have you heard of Times Square? Where is it? Why is it well known?

2 You're going to read an article about Times Square. Match the questions on the left with the answers on the right.

a) Where is it?
b) What is it?
c) And at other times?
d) What's it named for?

1 The building there that used to belong to a huge New York newspaper.
2 On New Year's Eve, for example, it's a loud, brash, sweaty mass of seething humanity.
3 On a typical day, one of the most concentrated business and entertainment districts in the nation.
4 Between Broadway, Seventh Avenue, and 42nd Street.

3 Read the article and answer these questions:

a) What type of entertainment does Times Square offer?
b) What type of people go to Times Square?
c) What money-saving tip does the writer mention?

TIMES SQUARE

(1) _____ , Times Square is one of the busiest spots in the largest city of the United States. With its huge business district, comprising 21 million square feet of office space and about 2 million more under construction, Times Square is home to approximately 1,500 businesses and organizations. Almost 26 million tourists visit Times Square annually, with 3.9 million overnight stays in the 12,500 hotel rooms in the area each year and millions more visits to the area's nearly 300 eateries.

The huge variety of attractions in Times Square attracts all types (2) _____ —young people and old people, natives and tourists, commoners and movie stars. The action in Times Square begins at dawn, as tourists wait outside the set of morning news shows such as Good Morning America to catch a glimpse of some of their favorite celebrities (3) _____ . Throughout the day, tourists visit shops, newsstands, bars, and restaurants. One of the main attractions, of course, is Broadway, "The Great White Way," with ticket prices ranging from economical to exorbitant—(4) _____ . But wise tourists know that TKTS sells tickets for nearly 50 percent off the regular price for same-day performances. Later, (5) _____ , the hustle and bustle continue as clubs and bars open their doors to the night life.

But the one day each year on which Times Square has the most visitors is December 31. (6) _____ , about a million people congregate there to ring in the New Year with a special celebration during which the brilliant New Year's Eve ball, designed by Waterford Crystal, descends to mark the new year. (7) _____ , this Times Square ceremony has been a universally renowned tradition that signals the end of one year and the beginning of the next.

There are so many attractions in Times Square worth seeing that it's a good idea to check out the Times Square Visitors Center at 1560 Broadway, the city's first-ever multi-service tourist center, (8) _____ .

Although tourism in Times Square and the rest of New York City decreased tremendously after September 11, 2001, the city is rebounding due in great part to the resiliency of New Yorkers and the strong national spirit throughout the country.

4 Below are eight words and phrases that were in the original text. Insert them into the appropriate spaces (1–8).

a) from all over the world
b) On New Year's Eve
c) and maybe even be on TV for a few seconds
d) especially on Friday and Saturday nights
e) to make sure you get the most out of your trip
f) For about a century
g) Every day
h) into the hundreds of dollars

5 Work with a partner. Student A: Turn to page A69. Student B: Turn to page A71.

6 Work in small groups and discuss the following questions:

a) What is the busiest place at night where you live? What do people do there? Are there theaters and restaurants? Which places would you recommend?
b) Do you like to go out for the evening? Where do you go? What do you do? When was the last time you went out for the evening? Tell your group where you went and what you did.

City Life

1 Work with a partner and discuss this question:

Is life in the city more dangerous than life in the country?

Write a list of the main dangers of city life.

2 🔊 17 Listen to two friends talking about the city they live in. As you listen, answer the following questions:

a) Do they think they live in a particularly dangerous city?
b) How many dangers from your list do they mention?
c) Do they mention any other dangers?

3 Compare your answers with a partner and discuss these questions:

a) What precautions do they suggest you should take when walking home at night?
b) In what places do they suggest you should take special care with your bag or wallet? Why?
c) There seems to have been an increase in crime recently. What sort of crime?
d) Have the speakers been victims of crime themselves? What about their friends?
e) What exactly happened to the group of tourists?
f) What do they think the police could do to improve the situation?

4 Listen again and check your answers.

Adding emphasis

1 Which word from the box can be used to mean the following?

a) extremely
b) now that you mention it
c) only
d) very
e) to tell you the truth
f) right at that moment
g) to be honest
h) very recently
i) simply
j) totally

| just |
| really |
| actually |

2 Look at these short excerpts from the conversation. Complete each one with *just, really,* or *actually*.

a) …there are certain areas that you ____ know you wouldn't go into…
b) …____ , there have been a couple of stories in the papers recently about this string of muggings that's been going on.
c) …her wallet was snatched from her bag ____ as the train was coming into the station…
d) You have to be ____ careful there because there is a big crowd and a lot of pickpockets…
e) You don't ____ know what's going on…
f) …I know that's a terrible thing to say, but it's ____ money.
g) ____ , I think she thought they were going to stab her husband.
h) …but the sad thing was that they had ____ arrived…
i) She didn't lose anything ____ valuable …
j) I think they ____ need to know if a crime has happened.

3 🔊 18 Listen and check your answers. Where does the stress fall?

4 Write a paragraph using *just, really,* and *actually* at least once each. Show it to a partner so that he/she can figure out their meanings. Practice reading the paragraph with emphasis.

Discussion

Work in small groups. Discuss one of these sets of questions:

- Is your hometown a dangerous place to live in? Do you need to take precautions when you go out at night? Would you go out alone after ten o'clock? If you were a member of the opposite sex, do you think your answers would be the same?
- Do you take extra precautions when you travel? Why/Why not? Are cities more dangerous if you're a tourist? Why/Why not?
- Which of the following safety measures are used in your town: police patrols at night, closed-circuit TV cameras in public places, security guards on public transportation, street lighting all night? What other measures can be taken to make our cities safer?

An Urban Poem

Vocabulary 1 Work with a partner. Look at the following words and phrases taken from the poem you are about to read. Answer the questions that follow.

> a mute   a mate   to hug someone   a gut   to joy-ride
> mucky   to pinch something   to boot something or someone
> daft   to nick something   to flog something

a) There are two nouns that refer to people. Which one means *a partner*? Which one means *a person who cannot speak*?
b) One noun refers to a part of the body. Which part?
c) Which two verbs mean *to steal*?
d) Which verb means *to kick violently*?
e) Which verb describes a much more tender action?
f) Which verb means *to sell*?
g) Which verb means *to steal a car and drive it around just for fun*?
h) There are two adjectives. One is a British English word for *stupid*. The other means *dirty*. Which is which?

2 Some of the words above are particularly informal. They have been included in the questions below in **bold**. Discuss your answers to the questions with a partner.

a) Have you ever had anything **nicked** from your car?
b) Did you ever **pinch** toys or candy when you were a kid?
c) What would you do if you saw someone **booting** one of your **mates**?
d) Have you ever **flogged** anything at a flea market?
e) When was the last time you got really **mucky**?
f) Have you done anything **daft** lately?

Reading 1 Work in small groups. Look at the poem below and answer the questions.

a) The verses have been mixed up. Decide on an appropriate order.
b) Do you think the character in the poem is male or female? Which lines in the poem support your argument?

a) *It took some time. Reassembled in the yard, he didn't look the same. I took a run and booted him. Again. Again. My breath ripped out in rags. It seems daft now. Then I was standing alone amongst lumps of snow, sick of the world.*

b) *Boredom. Mostly I'm so bored I could eat myself. One time, I stole a guitar and thought I might learn to play. I nicked a bust of Shakespeare once, flogged it, but the snowman was strangest. You don't understand a word I'm saying, do you?*

c) *Better off dead than giving in, not taking what you want. He weighed a ton; his torso, frozen stiff, hugged to my chest, a fierce chill piercing my gut. Part of the thrill was knowing that children would cry in the morning. Life's tough.*

d) *The most unusual thing I ever stole? A snowman. Midnight. He looked magnificent; a tall, white mute beneath the winter moon. I wanted him, a mate with a mind as cold as the slice of ice within my own brain. I started with the head.*

e) *Sometimes I steal things I don't need. I joy-ride cars to nowhere, break into houses just to have a look. I'm a mucky ghost, leave a mess, maybe pinch a camera. I watch my gloved hand twisting the doorknob. A stranger's bedroom. Mirrors. I sigh like this – Aah.*

(Poem by Carol Ann Duffy, from *Selling Manhattan*, 1986)

32 UNIT 3 *City*

2 🔊 19 Listen to the poem being read and check your answers.

3 Discuss these questions with your group:
   a) Do you like the poem?
   b) What do you think the title of the poem is?
   c) How old do you think the character is? Find lines in the poem that support your argument.
   d) Where do you think the character lives?
   e) Why does he/she steal?
   f) Why does he/she steal a snowman?
   g) Why do people steal things they don't need?

4 Choose two phrases that you found particularly evocative. Explain why you chose them.

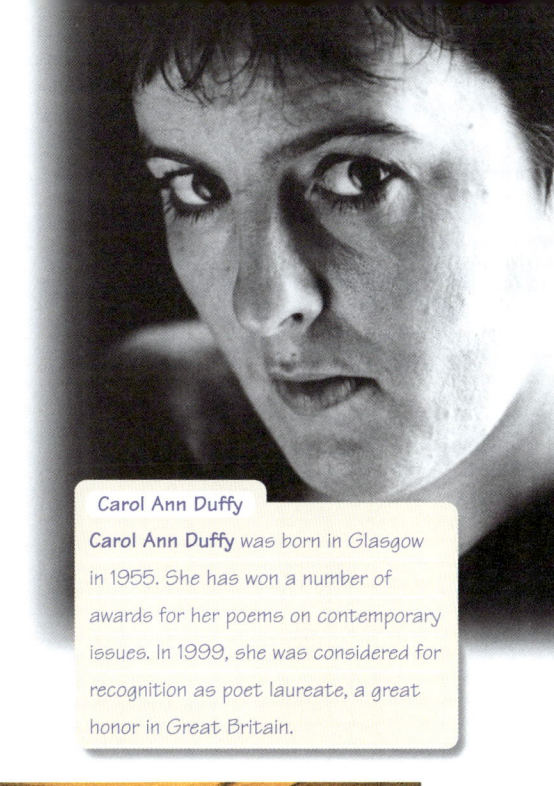

Carol Ann Duffy
Carol Ann Duffy was born in Glasgow in 1955. She has won a number of awards for her poems on contemporary issues. In 1999, she was considered for recognition as poet laureate, a great honor in Great Britain.

(Edward Hopper, *New York Movie*, 1939. MOMA, New York)

Discussion Work in small groups. Look at the painting and discuss these questions:
   a) Look at the woman in the painting. What do you think she's waiting for? What is she thinking? How does she feel?
   b) What are the three things that bore you most? Was it the same when you were a child?
   c) What do you do when you're bored? Do you just put up with it or do you do something to amuse yourself?

City **UNIT 3** 33

4 Talk

Find someone in the class who:

- is the most talkative member of his/her family.
- has spoken in front of a group of 50 people or more.
- has a job that involves listening.
- knows the difference between *whisper* and *whistle*.
- has gossiped about someone today.
- can say *I love you* in at least four languages.
- has had a conversation in English outside the classroom recently.

Conversation Piece

> **conversation**
>
> The word **conversation** is derived from the Latin verb **conversari,** which means "to keep company with". So, maybe what you talk about isn't as important as the fact that you are communicating.

1   Work in small groups. Define the word *conversation*. Do not use more than 20 words.

2   When you have agreed on the wording, look at the two dictionary definitions on page A72 and discuss these questions:
   a)   Which definition is more similar to your own?   b)   Which do you prefer?

3   Without looking back at the dictionary definitions, answer the following questions:
   a)   Is *conversation* countable, noncountable, or both?
   b)   Where is the main stress in *conversation*?
   c)   What's the difference between *having a conversation* and *making conversation*?
   d)   What three words can you form from the word *conversation*? Use them to complete these sentences.
      1   He's a great storyteller and an excellent ____ . He's never at a loss for words.
      2   She writes almost ____ . When you read her books, you can almost hear her talking to you.
      3   I don't want to learn how to read and write. ____ Japanese is enough for me.

4   Check your answers with the dictionary definitions.

5   Work with a partner and answer these questions:
   a)   What's the difference between *a chat, a conversation, a discussion,* and *an argument*?
   b)   Think of three more verbs to fill the blank: *to* ____ *(a) conversation*
   c)   What is the missing preposition in these expressions?
      1   they were deep ____ conversation
      2   she was engaged ____ conversation
      3   the subject came up ____ conversation

34   UNIT 4   *Talk*

6 Look at these adjectives that can be used to describe conversations.

> animated   pointless   overheard   riveting   lengthy   memorable
> frustrating   enjoyable   meaningful   predictable   boring   ~~recent~~
> one-way   fascinating   in-depth   hilarious

a) Classify the adjectives under the headings below.
b) Add two more adjectives under each heading and compare your answers with a partner.

positive	negative	neutral
		recent

7 *Conversational* is a graded adjective. Work with a partner and answer these questions:

a) Which of the adjectives in 6 can be graded with adverbs such as *very* or *fairly*?
b) Which of the adjectives cannot be graded?
c) What about the adjectives you added?

8 Think about the last time you had a conversation in English. Work with a partner and discuss these questions. Use adjectives from 6 if appropriate.

a) Who were you talking to? Did you know the person/people well?
b) Where were you?
c) What did you talk about?
d) Were you happy with your English?
e) Who did most of the talking, you or the other person/people?
f) How did the conversation end?

9 Find three things your conversations had in common.

The Art of Conversation

*Oh hello, George.
We were just talking about you.*

1 Work in small groups and discuss these questions:

a) What makes a conversation enjoyable?
b) What makes a conversation frustrating?
c) What's your definition of a good conversationalist?

2 Compare your answers with the rest of the class.

3 20 You are going to hear six people answering one of the questions in 1. As you listen, take brief notes on their answers. Use your notes to decide which question each one is answering.

speaker	notes	question answered
1	take active part, people who don't hog conversation	a

4 Compare your notes with a partner. Did the people interviewed have similar opinions to those expressed by your class?

Vocabulary

1 Look at these excerpts from the speakers' answers. Complete as many of the sentences as you can before you listen again.

a) …it helps if there aren't some people who (1) _____ the conversation all the time, and also people need to have a sense of humor about things, I think, not to take things too seriously, and you need a conversation that (2) _____…

b) …it's someone who has a point that they want to (3) _____ _____ during the conversation—someone with (4) _____ _____ _____ as opposed to someone who just talks nonstop about various subjects…

c) …also, some people don't care about whose (5) _____ it is to talk, so they just, you know, (6) _____ _____ when you're in the middle of a thought…

d) I really hate it when I'm with someone who just (7) _____ _____ _____ _____ in a conversation and who doesn't give you a chance to speak at all.

e) …like you're on (8) _____ _____ _____ , and you can share the same tastes or experiences so you know where the other person's coming from.

f) I can't stand it when you have to (9) _____ _____ _____ _____ yourself, when the other person's not responding, or when they are responding but it's with (10) _____ _____ , you know, just going yeah, uh, uhm, and that's all you're getting back, and when you have to work to (11) _____ _____ _____ _____ , that's really bad, when you're having to (12) _____ _____ for things to say…

2 Listen again and check your answers.

3 Work in small groups. Choose one of the questions below and discuss it with your group, using some of the expressions from 1.

a) Who is the best conversationalist you know? What makes him/her such a good conversationalist?
b) Can you remember a frustrating conversation you've had recently. Why was it so frustrating?
c) What was the most enjoyable conversation you've had recently? Who were you talking to? What made it so enjoyable?

Conversational Styles

1 You are going to read an article about conversational styles. Read the title and the first paragraph and answer these questions:

Who do you identify with, Sara or Betty? Why?

2 Read the rest of the article and decide what the topic of each section is. Match the headings below to the numbered sections.

a) Don't Take It Too Personally
b) Whose Turn Is It, Anyway?
c) It Depends on Where You Come From
d) Pause to Think
e) You Are What You Say

36 UNIT 4 *Talk*

"HOLD YOUR HORSES!" "WHAT ARE YOU WAITING FOR?"

PACING & PAUSING

Sara tried to befriend her old friend Steve's new wife, but Betty never seemed to have anything to say. While Sara felt Betty didn't hold up her end of the conversation, Betty complained to Steve that Sara never gave her a chance to talk. The problem had to do with expectations about pacing and pausing.

Conversation is a turn-taking game. You talk, then I talk, then you talk again. One person starts talking when another is finished. That seems simple enough.

1

But how do you know when I'm finished? Well, when I stop. But how do you know when I'm stopping? When my voice gets softer, when I start repeating myself, or when I slow down and pause at the end.

But how soft does my voice have to get to mean "That's about it" as opposed to "This isn't the main point yet" or "I'm a mumbler"? Does repeating myself mean "I'm out of new things to say" or "I'm emphasizing"? And how much of a pause after a word means "I'm stopping" as opposed to "I'm pausing within my turn"—pausing for breath, to find the right words, for dramatic effect, or, as any conversational signal, just out of habit?

2

In the midst of a conversation, you don't take time to puzzle this out. You sense when I'm finished, or about to make a point, or chatting aimlessly, based on your years of experience talking to people. When our habits are similar, there's no problem. What you sense and what I feel are similar. But if our habits are different, you may start to talk before I'm finished—in other words, interrupt—or fail to take your turn when I am finished—leading me to observe that you're not paying attention or have nothing to say.

That's what was happening with Betty and Sara. The tiny pause Betty was waiting for never occurred when Sara was around, because before it did, Sara would sense an awkward silence and would kindly end it by filling the pause with more talk—hers. And when Betty did start to say something, she would tend to have what seemed to Sara like long pauses within her speech, giving Sara the impression that Betty had finished when she had hardly gotten started.

Such differences are not a matter of some people expecting long pauses and others expecting short ones. Long and short are relative; they have meaning only in comparison to something—what's expected, or someone else's pause. Someone who expects a shorter pause than the person she's speaking to will often start talking before the other has a chance to finish or to start. Someone who is waiting for a longer pause than the person she's speaking to won't be able to get a word in edgewise.

3

It may not be coincidental that Betty, who expected relatively longer pauses between turns, is British, and Sara, who expected relatively shorter pauses, is American. Although there are group and individual differences among British and among American speakers, on the average, British speakers tend to expect longer pauses between turns than do Americans.

Betty often felt interrupted by Sara. But Betty herself became an interrupter and found herself doing all the talking when she met a visitor from Finland. Whereas she expected longer pauses between turns than Sara, she expected shorter pauses than the Finn. And Sara, who became interrupting and dominating in conversation with Betty, had a hard time getting a word in edgewise with some speakers from Latin America or Israel.

4

Differences among speakers from different countries are most pronounced and most easily identifiable. But there are also ethnic, regional, class, age, and gender differences among speakers from each country. And when members of one group can't get a conversation going with members of a certain other group, the result is often the stereotype that people from the other group are taciturn, uncooperative, or dull-witted. The British, for example, think of Scandinavians as being taciturn, but among Scandinavians, the Finns have a reputation for being slow and dull. Conversely, Americans from faster-speaking regions, like New York, are thought of as pushy, overbearing, and aggressive.

5

The general phenomenon, then, is that the small, automatic mechanisms for conversation, like pacing and pausing, lead people to draw conclusions not about conversational style but about personality and abilities. These habitual differences are often the basis for dangerous stereotyping. And these social phenomena can have very personal consequences. For example, a woman from the southwestern part of the United States went to live in an eastern city for a job in personnel. When the personnel department got together for meetings, she kept searching for the right time to break in—and never found it. Although back home she was considered outgoing and confident, in Washington she was perceived as shy and retiring. When she was evaluated at the end of a year, she was told to take an assertiveness-training course because of her inability to speak up.

That's why slight differences in conversational style—tiny little things like microseconds of pause—can have an enormous impact on your life. These little signals make up the mechanics of conversation, and when they're even slightly off, the conversation is thrown off—or even cut off. The result in this case was a judgment of psychological problems—even in the mind of the woman herself, who really wondered what was wrong with her and signed up for assertiveness training. ■

(Adapted from *That's Not What I Meant*, by Deborah Tannen, 1992)

3 Answer these questions:

a) What exactly was causing the problems between Sara and Betty?
b) Where were the two women from? Why is this significant?
c) How would you summarize the article to someone who hasn't read it?

4 Work with a partner and compare your answers.

Talk

5 Without looking back, decide whether each of these statements is true or false according to the article.

a) Betty didn't really have much to say to Sara.
b) The British tend to be quieter than Americans.
c) Israelis speak more quickly than most North Americans.
d) The Finns have a reputation for being boring.
e) New Yorkers take short pauses and tend not to wait for people to take their turn.
f) People from the east coast of the U.S. tend to speak a little more slowly than those from the southwest.
g) The way different nationalities speak contributes to the formation of national stereotypes.

6 Check your answers with the article and then discuss these questions with your partner:

a) The article is taken from a book. What type of reader is it written for?
b) Have you ever considered this topic before? Do you agree with the argument presented in the article?
c) Did the article make you think of anybody you know or any situations you've found yourself in?

Vocabulary

1 Match these words and phrases from the article with their definitions. Look back at the article if you need to check the meanings of the words.

a) never seemed to have anything to say (line 3/4)
b) didn't hold up her end of the conversation (line 5/6)
c) never gave her a chance to talk (line 7/8)
d) a mumbler (line 22)
e) chatting aimlessly (line 34)
f) interrupt (line 40)
g) an awkward silence (line 9)
h) had a hard time getting a word in edgewise (line 89/90)
i) can't get a conversation going (line 98)
j) inability to speak up (line 132/133)

1 talking about nothing in particular
2 unable to find a common subject of interest
3 say something which makes someone else stop what they are saying or doing
4 didn't contribute enough to the conversation
5 when neither person knows what to say, so no one says anything
6 dominated the conversation
7 lack of confidence at taking part in a conversation
8 was unable to express her point of view because she was not allowed time to speak
9 someone who doesn't speak clearly
10 was usually very quiet

2 Check your answers with a partner.

3 Work with a partner and discuss these questions:

a) Look back at the words and phrases (a–j) in 1. Which might be associated with Betty and which with Sara? Are there any that you would not associate with either?
b) Does the way people in your country speak vary from city to city or region to region?
c) Are you typical of your region or country?

Test Yourself

wh- words

1 Which word(s) in the box below refer(s) to

a) a point or period in time?
b) a place?
c) a reason?
d) a relationship of possession or belonging?
e) the way something is done?
f) a person?
g) a thing (2 words)?

| who | what | where | when | whose | which | why | how |

38 UNIT 4 *Talk*

2 Use the words in the box on page 38 to complete these sentences.

A (1) ____ you're talking to people (2) ____ don't really want to hear (3) ____ you have to say or (4) ____ keep interrupting you all the time and don't seem to care at all about (5) ____ turn it is to talk, it can be very disheartening.

B (6) ____ all you get is monosyllabic answers and you really don't know (7) ____ to keep the conversation going, you really have to hunt around for something to say, something (8) ____ 'll interest them and get them talking, and sometimes you wonder (9) ____ you even bother.

3 In how many places could you have used *that*?

4 Use words from 1 to complete the following questions:

a) ____ fault is it when a conversation breaks down?
b) Do you sometimes start talking without thinking about ____ you're going to say?
c) ____ is the best conversationalist you know?
d) Have you ever been in a situation ____ you've been at a loss for words?
e) ____ was the last time you said something and then wondered ____ you'd bothered?
f) ____ do you feel about talking to strangers?

5 Discuss the questions with a partner.

Eavesdropping

Secretly listening to other people's conversations is called *eavesdropping*. Work in small groups and discuss these questions:

a) In what kind of situations is it difficult not to eavesdrop?
b) What was the last conversation you eavesdropped on? Where were you? Who was talking? What were they talking about? Did they notice that you were listening to them?

Listening

1 🔊 21 You are going to "eavesdrop" on three conversations. As you listen, decide which conversation takes place

a) in a college dormitory room.   b) at a party.   c) in a restaurant.

2 In which conversation

a) did the speakers use to do something together?
b) have the speakers just started doing something together?
c) do the speakers share a similar problem?

3 Check your answers with a partner and discuss what the speakers are talking about in each conversation.

Vocabulary

1 Work with a partner. Look at the following expressions. They have all been taken from the conversations. Match them to definitions (1–6) on the right.

a) all sweetness and light
b) something catches my eye
c) take a break
d) a bite to eat
e) rant and rave
f) to live next door

1 a snack or a light meal
2 rest for a short time
3 to be neighbors
4 complain angrily about something
5 I have my attention drawn to something
6 smiling and happy

2 Which conversation does each expression come from? Listen again if necessary and check your answers.

3 Use the expressions in 1 on page 39 to complete these questions. Make any changes that are necessary.

a) Do you usually have a full meal at lunch time or do you just have ____ ?
b) Is your boss usually bad-tempered, or is he/she ____ ?
c) Do you get along well with the people who ____ to you?
d) Do you get a chance to ____ at all during the day, or are you always rushing around?
e) Is there anything that makes you really angry and makes you want to ____ ?
f) If a really expensive item of clothing ____ in a store window, do you go in and try it on or decide it's too expensive and walk away?

4 Choose three of the questions and ask your partner.

Close-up

General tendencies

1 Look at these short excerpts from the first two conversations. Write the correct form of each verb in parentheses.

a) ...he (1) ____ (rant and rave) for a while, and then half an hour later, he (2) ____ (forget) all about it. And then he (3) ____ (be) all sweetness and light after that.

b) ...sometimes after we (4) ____ (close), he (5) ____ (order) in some pizza for everybody, and then we (6) ____ (all sit around) talking and having a bite to eat.

c) ...I (7) ____ (go) and make a cup of coffee, and then I (8) ____ (just take) a break with my cup of coffee rather than work...

2 Compare your answers with a partner.

(Language Reference p. 41)

3 🎧 22 Listen and check your answers. Were your answers different from the recording? If yes, do you think your answers are also correct?

4 Which modal auxiliary is used in the excerpts? What time is this modal auxiliary usually associated with?

5 Look at these sentences and answer the questions that follow.

A He rants and raves for a while, and then he forgets all about it.
B He'll rant and rave for a while, and then he'll forget all about it.

a) Do the sentences refer to the present, the future, or no time in particular?
b) Which sentence is presenting a fact? Which mentions a tendency?

6 Complete the text below with the verbs in parentheses. Use *will* where possible.

If I (1) ____ (have) a really difficult project to do, say writing a particularly complex report or tackling a particularly difficult question, rather than getting down to it immediately, I (2) ____ (find) all kinds of little tasks to distract me. I (3) ____ (decide) that now is the perfect time to write all those letters to long lost friends, or I (4) ____ (start) cleaning the house from top to bottom. Sometimes I (5) ____ (do) some cooking, convincing myself that I (6) ____ (actually/save) time later by preparing all that food now. At other times I (7) ____ (spend) ages just staring out of the window and waiting for inspiration!

7 Work with a partner and discuss these questions:

a) Can you think of any other things people do to procrastinate when they don't want to do something?
b) Do you get things done right away, or do you tend to procrastinate?
c) If you are a procrastinator, what delaying tactics do you employ? If you aren't, do you know anybody who is? Describe how they put things off.

Tendencies in the past

1 Look at this excerpt from the third conversation. Write the correct form of each verb in parentheses.

Adam: Yes, the bus driver (1) ____ (wait) for me because he knew I (2) ____ (always be) a minute late.
Nick: And we (3) ____ (sit) at the back of the bus.
Adam: We (4) ____ . (*short answer*)
Nick: We had our little club for two.
Adam: That's right. And you, you (5) ____ (always forget) to do your homework, and you (6) ____ (have to) copy mine.
Nick: Yes. And do you remember you started me smoking? Remember we (7) ____ (go) down by the river and smoke at lunchtime?

2 Compare your answers with a partner.

Language Reference p. 41

3 🔊 23 Listen and check your answers. Were there any differences?

4 Work with a partner and discuss these questions:
   a) Which forms of the verb did you use in 1?
   b) Did you use *would* at all? If not, what verb form did you use in its place?
   c) What time does *would* refer to in the excerpt?
   d) Does *would* refer here to specific events or general tendencies?

5 Can *would* be replaced with the simple past in each of the following sentences? If not, say why.

   a) My grandfather would sit down with us and talk for hours on end, making up fabulous stories about characters he had invented on the spur of the moment. I wish I could remember them; then I would be able to tell them to my children.
   b) Our next-door neighbor was a terrible gossip. She would talk for hours and hours. If we'd given her the opportunity, she would have gone on forever!
   c) David used to be really shy as a child. He would be perfectly happy sitting quietly in the corner, playing contentedly by himself, and he hated having to talk to strangers.
   d) Sally was my best friend at college. She was the life of the party. She would always know the latest jokes and could tell them really well. Life in the dorm would have been very dull without her!

6 Do you know anyone like the people described above? Ask your partner.

Language Reference: Tendencies

We can use the modal auxiliaries *will* and *would* to talk about tendencies in general and tendencies in the past, respectively.

General tendencies

When we want to talk about facts that we think are generally true, we use the simple present.

The earth **revolves** around the sun.
The sun **rises** in the east and **sets** in the west.
The U.S. **consists** of fifty states plus the District of Columbia.

When we want to talk about things that generally tend to happen without suggesting that they always, inevitably happen, we can use the modal auxiliary *will*.

Men **will** often prefer to start a conversation about sports or the news, while women **will** talk about their feelings or their relationships.
You can tell her something one minute, and she**'ll** forget it the next.

Tendencies in the past

We can use *would* to talk about habits, tendencies, or characteristic behavior in the past.

*When I was young, my father **would** sit down with me in the kitchen every day after school and help me with my homework. On Saturday mornings we **would** go to the movies together, and he **would** let me go to the candy store on the way home. When we got back to the house, my mother **would** be waiting for us, and we **would** all have lunch together.*

We cannot use *would* to refer to a specific event in the past. We use the simple past for this.

*My father **would help** me with my homework last night.* ✗
*My father **helped** me with my homework last night.* ✓
*We **would see** a great movie at the new multiplex last weekend.* ✗
*We **saw** a great movie at the new multiplex last weekend.* ✓

I Love Them Dearly, But…

1 🔊 24 Listen to Ann talking about some of the members of her family, and answer the following questions:

a) Which members of the family does she mention? Write down their names and their relationship to her.
b) What habits and characteristics of theirs does she mention?

2 Work with a partner and check your answers. Then discuss these questions:

a) What do you think Ann's children might say about her? Do you think she may have some annoying habits or characteristics?
b) Does she remind you of anyone in your family?

Ann

Anecdote

1 You are going to tell your partner about a member of your family or a person you know, or used to know, very well. Look at the questions below. Which are you going to answer in your description? Think about the language you will need to use.

- ☐ How long have you known this person?
- ☐ What is his/her relationship to you?
- ☐ Does he/she have any annoying or endearing habits?
- ☐ Is there anything he/she used to do in the past but doesn't do anymore?
- ☐ What attracts you to this person?
- ☐ Have you had/Do you have any disagreements?
- ☐ What is his/her conversational style like?
- ☐ How does he/she approach life?
- ☐ Do you have anything in common?
- ☐ Is there anything else you'd like to add?

2 Tell your partner about the person.

3 When you have finished, look back at the questions listed above. Which did your partner include in his/her description? Did he/she mention anything else? Did your two descriptions have anything in common?

Talk

Vocabulary

1 Work with a partner. Look at the list below. It shows some of the most common uses and forms of the word *talk*. Which part of speech is used in each sentence—noun (countable or noncountable?), verb, or adjective?

A	Sitting next to Elaine was a small man who was **talking** intently to the woman on his left. *verb*
B	My mother has **talked** of nothing else since meeting you.
C	The next stage in the process will be **talks** between the American and Russian representatives.
D	I was already hearing **talk** about the merger of the two companies.
E	If you want to **talk** to me, call me "Sir"!
F	Morris gave a riveting **talk** on his visit to South Africa.
G	He's not very **talkative**, but you certainly feel his presence.
H	She has become the **talk** of the town since her very public relationship with the mayor.
I	If we're lucky, she'll stop **talking** to us altogether.
J	Simon was always late, despite always **talking** about family and responsibility.
K	I'm going to cover three areas in this brief **talk**, which most of you should find relevant.
L	After dinner we listened to Fred's hilarious **talk** about how to avoid becoming a millionaire.
M	During the meeting, the main **talking** point was the threat of downsizing.
N	You have no right to **talk**! You never exercise, and you smoke too much!
O	All that **talk** of food made me feel extremely hungry.
P	There's fresh **talk** of a strike at the car factory.

2 Use the sentences in 1 to help you answer these questions.

   a) Complete each of these expressions with an appropriate preposition:
      1 to talk ____ someone ____ something
      2 to give a talk ____ something
   b) What does *She was the talk of the town* mean?
   c) In what situation would you say *You have no right to talk!*?
   d) Complete each of these sentences, using one of the forms of *talk*:
      1 Are there any international peace ____ going on these days?
      2 When did you last go to a public ____ ? What was it on?
      3 Who's the most ____ person you know?
      4 What's the main ____ point in today's meeting?
   e) What is the difference between these three nouns: *talks, a talk,* and *talk*?

3 Work with a partner. Discuss the questions in 2d.

Joke Time

Stress

1 You are going to hear a comedian telling a story containing these four items:

Work with a partner. Discuss how you think the items might be linked. Tell your story to the class.

2 🔊 25 Listen to the story. Is it different from your version? Do you think it is funny? Why/Why not?

3 One of the important things about telling a joke successfully is getting the timing and pace of delivery right. Turn to page A69 to take a closer look at how this joke is told.

Doctor! Doctor!

1 Below are the first lines of three jokes. Match each one with the two other lines to make a three-line joke.

   a) A man goes to see his doctor and says, "Doctor! Doctor! I can't stop shaking."
   b) A man says to his doctor, "Doctor! Doctor! Will I be able to play the violin after the operation?"
   c) A man speaks frantically into the phone, "Doctor! Doctor! My wife is pregnant, and her contractions are only two minutes apart!"

   1 "No, you idiot!" the man shouts. "This is her husband."
   2 And the man replies, "Not really; I spill most of it!"
   3 "Great!" the man says. "I never could before!"
   4 "Is this her first child?" the doctor asks.
   5 The doctor asks him, "Do you drink a lot?"
   6 "Yes, of course," replies the doctor.

2 Check your answers with a partner and then practice reading the jokes aloud. Pay particular attention to pace and timing.

3 Work with a partner and discuss your answers to these questions:

   a) Which is your favorite joke in 1? Which made you laugh? Which made you groan?
   b) Do you have "Doctor! Doctor!" jokes in your language? What kind of jokes are common these days? Can they be translated, or do they depend on a play on words?

5 Luck

1 Good-luck charms vary from country to country. Match the charms with the countries in the box.

rabbit's foot   scarab   dragon   peacock feathers   horn

| Turkey | Egypt | Italy | China | United States | India |

2 🔊 26 Listen and check your answers.

3 Work with a partner and answer these questions:

a) What are considered good-luck charms in your country? What is considered to bring bad luck?
b) Do you have a good-luck charm? Are you lucky? Have you ever won anything? If so, what?
c) Do you ever play the lottery? If you do, how do you choose your numbers? What's the most you've ever won? If you don't play, why not?
d) What would you do if you won "the big one"?

Winning "the Big One"

1 Read the article from *People* magazine and answer these questions:

a) How do some people usually choose their lottery numbers? How would/do you choose lottery numbers?
b) What advice would you give a person who has won a huge amount of money?
c) Which do you think is the best subtitle for the article?
Money Is Everything
Dreams Can Come True
Hitting the Jackpot

2 Compare your answers with a partner.

People

People is a weekly American magazine that contains newsy articles about celebrities as well as ordinary people who have done extraordinary things— like win the lottery.

AFTER THE JACKPOT

Shock, elation, and phone calls from long-lost cousin Ed: Lottery winners tell how they coped with windfall wealth.

Just pencil in your birthday plus your high school locker combination, plunk down a buck or maybe 50, cross your fingers and... next thing you know you're sipping mai tais in the Jacuzzi of your stretch Mercedes SUV. Never mind that you're ten times more likely to be killed by a bee sting—winning a whopping lottery jackpot is still the quickest, easiest way to realizing the American Dream.

Or is it? Sure, today's lottery jackpots are growing faster than Tobey Maguire's asking price, producing some gargantuan payouts. Just look at 20-year old Erika Greene, who last month pulled up to the Georgia lottery office in a limousine to cash her $58.9 million Big Game lottery ticket. "People used to get excited about $20 million or $30 million," says Chuck Strutt, executive director of the Multi-State Lottery Association, which created the first Powerball jackpot in 1992. "Now it takes $50 to $100 million before we get national attention." But with massive windfalls can come major headaches, such as needy, distant relatives who suddenly remember your phone number. "You get bombarded with some outrageous requests, like 'Uncle Ray needs a new leg.'" says Bob Hainey, a Washington, DC, lottery manager. "You've got to put up a firewall, or you can get cash-poor pretty quickly."

Your best bet: Hire a good financial planner, take a deep breath before buying that minor-league baseball team, and listen to what the following big winners have to say about what happens after you hit the jackpot.

Mary Champaine
Amount won: $6.6 million

For a few years, Mary Champaine suffered an epic streak of misfortune. In April 1997, a stray bullet from warring Los Angeles gangs killed her 24-year-old stepson, Al; a year later she lost her mother-in-law and father; in August 1999, the firm where she had worked as a personnel trainer folded; a month later her husband Albert, 50, succumbed to cancer. Recalls Champaine, now 55, who found work as a Starbucks manager weeks after her husband's death, "I was too busy surviving to grieve over my losses."

Then in October 2000, one of the 13 tickets Champaine had bought for herself and her employees in the California Super Lotto Plus won an $87 million pot. Although Champaine's windfall made her an overnight celebrity, she continued at her $32,000-a-year job until December 2000. "It just got crazy," she says. "I heard so many sales pitches that it made me tremble."

She kept her head, though: Her first purchases were a glass doorknob and a dimmer switch (she installed them herself) for her modest home in East L.A. Next year she plans to build a house for her daughter, Michelle Brandon, 30, and two grandchildren. Champaine, who had heart surgery in July 2002, now walks every day at dawn and takes belly-dancing lessons with a friend. "Money doesn't make you happy," Champaine says. "What makes me happy is that my granddaughters are going to be able to go to college."

Paul Cooney
Amount won: $20.7 million

Attention, future lottery winners: Before spending a penny, consider the cautionary tale of Paul Cooney. Since scoring $20.7 million in the Florida lottery in '89, Cooney—a former dispatcher at a Georgia Ford dealership—has racked up a collection of missteps almost as formidable as his fortune. Among them: purchasing a failing Chrysler dealership; investing in a now-shuttered Italian restaurant; divorcing his wife of nearly 11 years; remarrying in '96 and divorcing his second wife in '97; and, finally, filing for Chapter 11 bankruptcy in '99. Looking back, Cooney, 39, says, "I was 26; what I did was too softhearted." After repaying most of his debts, Cooney is about to break even, though he continues to shell out half of his annual $1,035,000 lottery award in alimony to his first ex-wife, Donna, 40. Despite his mistakes, he notes, things could be worse: After all, "I still get my checks. I get $517,000 a year gross."

(From *People*, June 10, 2002)

---

3 Work with a partner. Discuss these questions:

a) In what ways has winning the California Super Lotto Plus changed Mary Champaine's life? Do you think winning so much money has made up for the hardships she suffered in the past?
b) How has winning the lottery made life better for these people? How has it made life worse?
c) What advice would you give to a person who has become instantly rich?
d) If you had won the most recent big lottery in your country, what would you have done with the money?

I Almost Won

In a little convenience store in Maine, Bertha Reed, 76, a weekly lottery player, tells everyone who comes into the store how she almost hit "the big one."

"I'm telling you folks, last week I had all the numbers except one. Can you believe that? One number off. It's because I didn't play my usual numbers. I had it all planned. A diamond-studded collar for my poodle. A snazzy new car for me. And gorgeous new clothes for me too. And maybe a new boyfriend. Wait until next week. I'll never give up!"

Then next week comes, and Bertha tells the same story. Oh, well, maybe next time!

(From *Living Large*)

Vocabulary   **1**   The writer of the article assumes the reader has certain background knowledge. Take this quiz and see how much you know.

Quiz

1. *Locker combination* (line 2) refers to…
   a) directions.
   b) dates.
   c) numbers.

2. A *Jacuzzi* (line 5) is…
   a) an expensive car.
   b) a hot tub.
   c) an expensive watch.

3. The letters *SUV* (line 6) stand for…
   a) super utility van.
   b) sport utility vehicle.
   c) super united van.

4. *Tobey Maguire* (line 11) is…
   a) an actor in *Spiderman*.
   b) an actress in *Spiderman*.
   c) a famous lottery winner.

5. *Starbucks* (line 44) refers to…
   a) a coffee bar chain.
   b) a supermarket chain.
   c) a restaurant chain.

6. A *cautionary tale* (line 69) is…
   a) a story of good luck.
   b) a story that warns by example.
   c) a story that gives hope.

7. A *Chrysler dealership* (line 75) is…
   a) a car financing group.
   b) an auto manufacturer.
   c) a franchise that sells cars.

8. *Gross* (line 87) means…
   a) before taxes are paid.
   b) after taxes are paid.
   c) on time.

2   Check your answers on page A68.

3   Find verbs on page 45 that mean:
   a) to write (paragraph 1)
   b) to gain or obtain something worthwhile (paragraph 1)
   c) to drive a vehicle to a specified place (paragraph 2)
   d) to die (paragraph 4)
   e) to shake involuntarily (paragraph 5)
   f) to fix in position for use (paragraph 6)
   g) to collect or accumulate (paragraph 7)
   h) to finish as neither a winner nor a loser (paragraph 7)
   i) to pay out money, usually a large amount (paragraph 7)
   j) to mention particularly (paragraph 7)
   k) to stop doing something (paragraph 9)

Underline the two-word verbs.

4   Which verbs in 3 can involve the eyes, the hands, the whole body, or the voice?

5   Use the verbs in 3 in an appropriate form to complete these sentences.
   a) It was very difficult ____ the new electric stove.
   b) When she heard the news that her husband had won the lottery, she began ____ all over.
   c) I ____ his name in my appointment book for lunch on Friday at 1 o'clock.
   d) Shaquille was ____ point after point during the championship basketball game against the Nets.
   e) He put up a good fight but unfortunately ____ to the disease.
   f) I would have ____ my dream to become an actress if only I had had some acting talent.
   g) The couple ____ to the castle gates in their old beat-up 1983 Ford.
   h) This has been a terrible year for my business, so I'm sure I'm not going ____ .
   i) The speaker ____ that this was the first time that he had ever talked to such a large audience.
   j) I know that someday I will win "the big one." I'll never ____ !
   k) The man felt very resentful after he had ____ $500 for the dinner for only four people.

6   Tell your partner about the last time you or someone you know did two of the things in 5.

UNIT 5   Luck

Close-up

Unreal conditionals

1 🔊 27 Listen to a conversation between Sarah and Angela, who have just read the *People* article and the article about Bertha. Answer these questions:

a) Which parts of the articles did they enjoy in particular?
b) Do they play the lottery?
c) Has either of them ever won anything?

2 Compare your answers with a partner.

3 Look at these excerpts from the conversation and complete the sentences.

Sarah and Angela

EXCERPT 1

Sarah: Did you read that article in *Living Large* about Bertha? It's a good story.
Angela: Yeah, and all that stuff about what (1) ____ if (2) ____ "the big one."
Sarah: Yeah, I really like that part about how (3) ____ her dog's life, like (4) ____ a diamond-studded collar right now…
Angela: Nah, I think it's more likely that (5) ____ a snazzy little red sports car!

EXCERPT 2

Sarah: I got really close to winning once. If (6) ____ my brother's birthday instead of mine, (7) ____ .
Angela: How much (8) ____ if (9) ____ ?
Sarah: Oh, millions, probably. I (10) ____ a new house, a car, and a yacht, and I (11) ____ as an editorial assistant anymore, I can tell you!

4 Listen again and check your answers.

Language Reference p. 48

5 Work with a partner and answer the questions below.

Excerpt 1
a) Is a real or an unreal situation being described?
b) Find one possible past result of the situation.
c) Find two possible present results.

Excerpt 2
a) Is a real or an unreal situation being described?
b) Find one possible past result of the situation.
c) Find one possible present result.

6 Write out the correct form of the verbs in parentheses.

a) If I ____ (stay in) last night, I ____ (not be) so tired today.
b) If I ____ (not/work) late last night, I ____ (go) to the movies.
c) If I ____ (go) to bed earlier, I ____ (not/get up) so late.
d) If I ____ (sleep) a little later, I ____ (not/yawn) now.

7 Look at the sentences again. What other modal auxiliaries can you use instead of *would*?

8 Are any of the sentences in 6 true for you? If not, change them to make them true and compare your sentences with a partner.

Luck UNIT 5

9 Look at these sentences and answer the questions that follow.

Had the writer chosen her numbers differently, her life might have changed dramatically.
Had I complained to the manager, I would have had my money refunded.

   a) How are these sentences different in structure from the ones in 6 on page 47?
   b) Which structure is more formal?

10 Complete these sentences so they are true for you.

   a) Had I…
   b) Had I had…
   c) Had I been…

Language Reference: Unreal conditionals

The *if* clause (describing an unreal situation)

To describe a past situation that is unreal, or imagine how a past situation might have been different, we backshift the verb in the *if* clause.

What really happened (real past)		What might have happened (unreal past)
She **won** a small amount of money in the lottery.	→	If she **had won** the jackpot…
She **wasn't paying** attention.	→	If she **had been paying** a little more attention…

Substituting *if*

Instead of using *if* to introduce the unreal situation, we can invert the subject and verb.

If she had won the jackpot… → **Had** she won the jackpot…
If your work had been more satisfactory… → **Had** your work been more satisfactory…

This is formal language, especially if it is written.

The main clause

Describing possible present consequences
We use *would (do)* or *would be (doing)* to describe the **possible present consequences** of the unreal past situation.

If she **had won** the lottery, she **wouldn't be working** anymore.
If she **had been paying** more attention, she **wouldn't be** in such a mess.

Describing possible past consequences
We use *would have (done)* or *would have been (doing)* to describe the **possible past consequences** of the unreal past situation.

If she **had won** the lottery, she **would have bought** a snazzy red sports car.
She **wouldn't have been daydreaming** in class if the lesson **had been** a little more interesting.

The *if* clause and the main clause can be used in either order.

A Lucky Break

1 Look at the pictures. What do you think the story is that connects them?

2 28 Listen to Louise telling her story. How similar was your story?

UNIT 5 *Luck*

3 Answer these questions about the story:

  a) Who first noticed the thieves?
  b) How were the thieves caught?
  c) Whose idea was it?
  d) How do you think the thieves felt?

Close-up

Wishes and regrets

1 Match the first part of the sentences on the left with the endings on the right.

  a) I bet the thieves wished they'd
  b) Kelly wishes she'd
  c) The girls wished they hadn't

  1 kept an eye on her coat while she was in the restaurant.
  2 spent so long talking.
  3 turned the phone off.

What do you notice about the verb structure that follows these wishes and regrets?

2 What other wishes or regrets might the people in the story have had?

Language Reference p. 50

3 Match the two parts of the sentences in the three groups below.

1
  a I wish I loved you,
  b I wish I didn't love you,
  c I wish I could love you,

  1 but hard as I try, I can't.
  2 but I don't.
  3 but the fact is, I do.

2
  a I wish you had left
  b I wish you would leave,
  c I wish you weren't leaving

  1 because you're getting on my nerves.
  2 so early.
  3 before my mother arrived.

3
  a I wish I had told you,
  b I wish I could tell you,
  c I wish I hadn't told you,

  1 but I promised I wouldn't tell anyone.
  2 because I didn't know you'd be so upset.
  3 but I was scared you'd get mad at me.

4 Look at the sentences again and answer these questions.

  a) Which three sentences express a definite wish to change the past?
  b) Which two sentences express a definite wish to change the present?
  c) Which four sentences express a desire to change the near future or the present?

5 Which verb forms are used in cases a–c in 4?

6 Finish these sentences so they are true for you. Discuss your sentences with a partner.

  a) I wish I (simple past)…
  b) I wish I had …
  c) I wish… (past continuous)
  d) I wish…would…
  e) I wish…could…

Regrets

Language Reference p. 50

1 Which of these sentences are incorrect? Make changes to them so they are correct.

a) I regret leaving my job last year.
b) If only I spent so much money last weekend.
c) I regret to have that argument with my best friend.
d) I regret not having learned to play a musical instrument.
e) If only I'd gotten up so late this morning.
f) I regret not going to Spain on vacation last year.
g) I regret having lent my car to my brother.
h) I regret not to take my driving test.
i) If only I'd gotten through my work more quickly.

2 Are any of the regrets in 1 true for you? Tell your partner about them.

Game

Wishful Thinking
Work in small groups. Think of a famous person, cartoon, or fairytale character. Write down three possible wishes or regrets that this person or character might have expressed. Read your wishes to the rest of the class to guess who it is.

Language Reference: Wishes and regrets

We backshift the verb after *wish* to express the following unreal (and wished for) situations.

Regrets about past situations
I **didn't tell** you the truth. → I wish that **I'd told** you the truth.
I **wasn't** really **concentrating**. → I wish **I'd been concentrating**.

Regrets about present situations
I **don't have** enough time to study. → I wish **I had** more time to study.
You**'re working** very hard these days. → I wish that you **weren't working** so hard.

A desire to change the future
They**'re coming** to visit us next weekend. → I wish they **weren't coming** to visit us next weekend.

I**'m going to** fail my exam again. → I wish I **weren't going to** fail my exam again.

In clauses after *wish*, we usually use *were/weren't* where we would normally use *was/wasn't*. *Wasn't* is usually used only in informal speech.

Could is also used to emphasize the inability to change a situation in the present or future.
I wish I loved you. (but I don't)
I wish I **could** love you. (but I can't)

We can also use *would* to describe a desired change in the present or future. It emphasizes a sense of longing or irritation.

It **isn't raining**. → I wish it **would rain**.
You **smoke** in the house. → I wish (that) you **wouldn't smoke** in the house.

In informal clauses with *wish*, *that* can be omitted.

Other ways of expressing regret

if only + past perfect
If only I'd studied English when I was younger.
If only I hadn't eaten the whole pizza!

regret + *-ing*
The verb that follows *regret* is always in the *-ing* form whether it is an auxiliary or not.
I **regret choosing** French when I was at school.
I **regret not having studied** English when I was younger.

Notes:
We use *wish* + infinitive to express a formal intention. This form is usually used in writing.
We **wish to inform** you that the offices will be closed on Mondays until further notice.
We **wish to congratulate** you on your recent success.
We **wish to thank** all those who participated in the recent conference.

We can also use the verb *regret* + infinitive in a formal context to say that we are sorry about something. It is often used to break bad news.
We **regret to inform** you that you have failed the exam.
I **regret to announce** that Paul will be leaving the company at the end of the month.

UNIT 5 *Luck*

Wish Fulfillment

Vocabulary

1 Look at this list of song titles with *wish* in them. Have you heard of any of the songs or artists? Which title do you like the best? Which is the most romantic title? Which is the saddest title?

SINGSEARCH

You searched for: wish

Sing Search found the following matches:

Title	Artist
I Wish Every Day Could be Like Christmas	Bon Jovi
I Wish We Could be Alone	Laura Branigan
I Wish I Didn't Love You So	kd Lang
I Wish It Would Rain	The Temptations
I Wish That I Could Fall in Love Today	Barbara Mandrell
I Wish That I Could Tell You	Reba McEntire
I Wish the Phone Would Ring	Expose
I Wish You Could be Here	The Seekers
I Wish You Love	Paul Young
I Wish You Peace	The Eagles
I Wish You Well	Tom Cochrane
King of Wishful Thinking	Go West
My Wish Came True	Elvis Presley
You Can Make a Wish	Mica Paris
Wish Fulfillment	Sonic Youth
Wish List	Pearl Jam
Wish You Were Here	Pink Floyd
Wishing Well	Black Sabbath

2 Work with a partner. Look through the list again and answer these questions:

a) What part of speech is *wish* and the words formed from it in each title?
b) Find two adjectives formed from the root *wish*. What nouns do they form an expression with?
c) The noun *wish* is used to describe other nouns. Find two examples.
d) Find an example of each of these patterns:
   I wish + clause
   I wish you + adverb
   I wish you + noun

3 Write some song titles, using the cues below. Use your imagination!

a) wish/phone/ring
b) wish/fly/eagle
c) wish/tell/truth
d) wish/all the money in the world
e) wish/somewhere else
f) wish/you/me

4 Complete each of these questions with an appropriate verb and discuss them with your partner.

a) In the U.S. it is traditional to ____ a wish when you blow out candles on a birthday cake. Do you have the same, or a similar, tradition in your country?
b) If you could ____ three wishes now, what would they be?
c) Have any of your wishes ever ____ true?

Luck UNIT 5

Anecdote　　1　You're going to tell your partner about an event or an important period in your life that has influenced the way you are today. Before you tell your partner, think about these questions and the language you will use.

- ☐ What was it? An accident? A vacation? A chance meeting? A stroke of luck or an unfortunate incident? An event at high school or college? A new job?
- ☐ How long ago was it?
- ☐ Exactly what happened?
- ☐ Why was it so important?
- ☐ How did it influence you? Did it influence you for the better or for the worse?
- ☐ Do you wish it had never happened, or are you glad that it did?
- ☐ How would your life be different if this event had not occurred? Would you have the same friends/job/character? Would your lifestyle be different?
- ☐ Is there anything else you'd like to add?

2　Tell your partner about the event.

3　Did your anecdotes have anything in common?

The Day of the Triffids

1　Work with a partner. Look at the picture, which illustrates part of the story you are going to hear. What do you think the story is about?

UNIT 5 *Luck*

2 🔊 29 Listen to some excerpts from the book *The Day of the Triffids*. Decide whether each of these sentences is true or false.

   a) The storyteller's whole body was in bandages.
   b) The storyteller knew something was wrong, because he couldn't hear any traffic.
   c) The storyteller was in a mental hospital.
   d) Somebody in the street was singing.
   e) On Tuesday, May 7, the Earth passed through some comet debris.
   f) The storyteller really enjoyed the fireworks.
   g) The storyteller opened the curtains for the patients in the surgical ward.
   h) A Triffid is a carnivorous animal capable of killing a man.

3 Work in small groups and answer these questions:

   a) How did the comet debris bring about "the end of the world"?
   b) How did the writer survive it?
   c) Why did he think that he might have been transferred to a mental hospital?
   d) When did he realize that all the other patients were blind?
   e) What made Triffids different from other plants?

4 Listen again and check your answers.

5 Work with a partner. Discuss these questions:

   a) What would some of the major consequences of practically everyone going blind be? The storyteller described it as "the end of the world." Do you think he was exaggerating?
   b) Approximately 99% of the population was blinded. Imagine that you and your partner were two of the lucky ones who weren't. How would you have spent that first Wednesday?

Three Months Later…

The Day of the Triffids starts off with the end of the world as we know it. This is caused by comet debris that blinds practically everyone. To add to everyone's difficulties, the Earth is also plagued by flesh-eating Triffids.

Work with a partner. Write the narrator's diary for the first three months of life after "the end of the world." Before you start writing, discuss the points below with your partner. Write about 100 words for each month.

The first month
Have you met other sighted people? How did you meet them? What do they do? Do you or they have skills that will be useful in this "new" life?
What has happened to the people who were blinded by the comet debris?
What is everyday life like? What about food, water, electricity? Do you still use money?
How are you dealing with the Triffids?
Are you still living in the same town or city, or have you had to move? Why?

The second month
Do you still get along with the other sighted people you've met? Do you share the same objectives for the future? What are they?
Have your food supplies run short? What are your plans for long-term food supplies?
Are the Triffids increasing in number, or have you found a way of reducing their numbers?
What medical problems have you had?

The third month
What do you do every day? Are your lives beginning to get into a routine?
What do the blind people do?
How are you feeling? Are you optimistic about the future? What do you think the future holds?

LANGUAGE TOOLBOX

Linking phrases
To start with, we…
At first, we didn't understand…
After a short period we began to…
Eventually, we realized that…
The next step was to…
After various attempts, we…
Although we tried to…
In spite of / Despite this…
Anyway, going back to…
Even though the Triffids have…
They… whereas / while we…

Luck UNIT 5 53

6 Mind

1 How much do you know about your brain? Answer true or false to each of these quiz questions and find out.

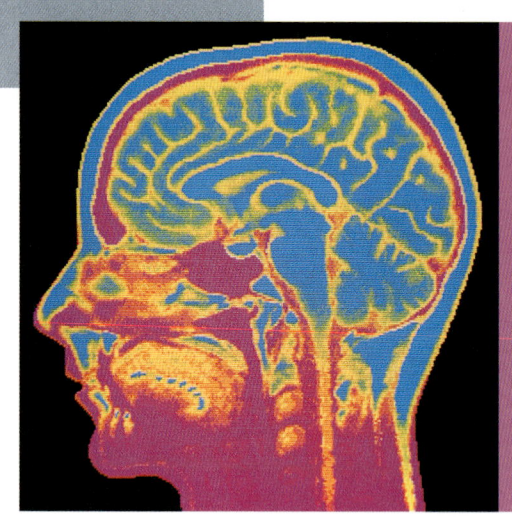

- **A** On average, the adult brain weighs 6.2 pounds in a man and 4.8 pounds in a woman.
- **B** The brain floats in a liquid in the skull.
- **C** 50% of the average human brain is water.
- **D** Your brain is uniformly pink in color.
- **E** The human adult brain uses up to 25% of the blood's oxygen supply.
- **F** We only use 10% of our brains.
- **G** Your brain cannot feel pain.
- **H** Your brain is more active watching TV than it is sleeping.
- **I** We yawn more when our brains are not being stimulated.
- **J** The human brain continues to send out electrical signals for up to 37 hours following death.

2 Check your answers on page A69.

Mind Matters

1 Work with a partner. Discuss these questions:

a) Have you read or heard about this book or Dr. Oliver Sacks?
b) What do you think the case called *The Man Who Mistook His Wife for a Hat* is about?

2 Read these four excerpts from the case and match these headings to them.

a) The Doctor's Examination   c) The Diagnosis
b) The Doctor's First Impression d) The Patient

The Man Who Mistook His Wife for a Hat is the title of a book concerning malfunctions of the brain. It was written by the neurologist Dr. Oliver Sacks. The title of the book is also the title of one of the cases.

The Man Who Mistook His Wife for a Hat

1

Dr. P. was a musician of distinction, well-known for many years as a singer, and then at the local school of music, as a teacher. It was here, in relation to his students, that certain strange problems were first observed. Sometimes a student would present himself, and Dr. P. would not recognize him—or, specifically, would not recognize his face. The moment the student spoke, he would be recognized by his voice. Such incidents multiplied, causing embarrassment, perplexity, fear—and, sometimes, comedy.
5 For not only did Dr. P. increasingly fail to see faces, but he saw faces when there were no faces to see: genially, when in the street, he might pat the heads of fire hydrants and parking meters, taking these to be the heads of children; he would amiably address carved knobs on the furniture and be astounded when they did not reply.

The notion of there being "something the matter" did not emerge until some three years later, when diabetes developed. Well aware that diabetes could affect his eyes, Dr. P. consulted an ophthalmologist, who took a careful history and examined his eyes
10 closely. "There's nothing the matter with your eyes," the doctor concluded. "But there is trouble with the visual parts of your brain. You don't need my help; you must see a neurologist." And so, as a result of this referral, Dr. P. came to me.

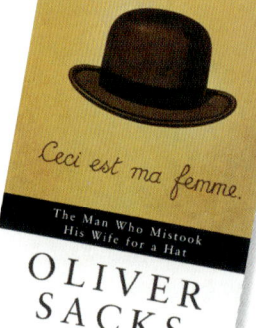

2

It was obvious within a few seconds of meeting him that there was no trace of dementia in the ordinary sense. He was a man of great cultivation and charm, who talked well and fluently, with imagination and humor. I couldn't think why he had been referred to our clinic.

And yet there was something a bit odd. He faced me as he spoke, was oriented toward me, and yet there was something the matter—it was difficult to formulate. He faced me with his ears, I came to think, but not with his eyes. These, instead of looking, gazing, at me, "taking me in," in the normal way, made sudden strange fixations—on my nose, on my right ear, down to my chin, up to my right eye—as if noting (even studying) these individual features, but not seeing my whole face, its changing expressions, "me," as a whole. I am not sure I fully realized this at the time—there was just a teasing strangeness, some failure in the normal interplay of gaze and expression. He saw me, he scanned me, and yet...

"What seems to be the matter?" I asked him at length.

"Nothing that I know of," he replied with a smile, "but people seem to think there's something wrong with my eyes."

"But you don't recognize any visual problems?"

"No, not directly, but I occasionally make mistakes."

3

He saw all right, but what did he see? I opened out a copy of *National Geographic*, and asked him to describe some pictures in it.

His responses here were very curious. His eyes would dart from one thing to another, picking up tiny features, individual features, as they had done with my face. A striking brightness, a color, a shape would arrest his attention and elicit comment—but in no case did he get the scene as a whole.

"What is this?" I asked, holding up a glove.

"May I examine it?" he asked, and, taking it from me, he proceeded to examine it.

"A continuous surface," he announced at last, "infolded on itself. It appears to have"—he hesitated—"five outpouchings, if this is the word."

"Yes," I said cautiously. "You have given me a description. Now tell me what it is."

"A container of some sort?"

"Yes," I said, "and what would it contain?"

"It would contain its contents!" said Dr. P., with a laugh. "There are many possibilities. It could be a change purse, for example, for coins of five sizes. It could..."

I interrupted the barmy flow. "Does it not look familiar? Do you think it might contain, might fit, a part of your body?"

No light of recognition dawned on his face.

No child would have the power to see and speak of "a continuous surface...infolded on itself," but any child, any infant, would immediately know a glove as a glove, see it as familiar, as going with a hand. Dr. P. didn't. He saw nothing as familiar. Visually, he was lost in a world of lifeless abstractions.

4

"Well, Dr. Sacks," he said to me. "You find me an interesting case, I perceive. Can you tell me what you find wrong, make recommendations?"

"I can't tell you what I find wrong," I replied, "but I'll say what I find right. You are a wonderful musician, and music is your life. What I would prescribe, in a case such as yours, is a life which consists entirely of music. Music has been the center, now make it the whole, of your life."

(Excerpts from *The Man Who Mistook His Wife for a Hat* by Oliver Sacks, 1985)

3 Work with a partner and discuss these questions:

a) What were Dr. P.'s first symptoms?
b) Why did Dr. P. consult an ophthalmologist? Why was the ophthalmologist unable to help him?
c) What did Dr. Sacks notice about Dr. P.'s eyes when they first met?
d) Was Dr. P. aware that he didn't see normally? Why/Why not?
e) How *did* Dr. P. see?
f) How do you think Dr. P. would describe a book or a pair of glasses? What might he mistake them for?
g) What advice did Dr. Sacks give the patient? Is this the kind of advice you would expect from a doctor? Why did he give him this advice?
h) Look at these titles of other case histories from the book. What do you think the problem was in each case?
The Lost Mariner
The Phantom Finger
The Dog Beneath the Skin
You can find out by reading the file cards on page A70.

Vocabulary

1 Find words in sentences 1–8 below with the following meanings:

a) looking steadily at something for a long time
b) noticed
c) move suddenly and quickly
d) understand something by looking at it
e) know what something is when you see it again
f) looked at or over something carefully or quickly
g) to look closely or analytically at something
h) become aware of something by using your eyes

1 It was here, in relation to his students, that certain strange problems were first observed. (line 2)
2 …Dr. P. would not recognize him—or, specifically, would not recognize his face. (line 3)
3 …instead of looking, gazing, at me, "taking me in," in the normal way… (lines 16–17)
4 He saw me, he scanned me, and yet… (line 20)
5 He saw all right, but what did he see? (line 25)
6 His eyes would dart from one thing to another… (line 27)
7 …taking it from me, he proceeded to examine it. (line 31)
8 You find me an interesting case, I perceive. (line 44)

2 *Observe, recognize,* and *see* have more than one meaning. Look at these sentences and match the verbs with the meanings in the box.

a) I recognize I'm not perfect.
b) I see what you mean.
c) They have recognized the importance of your contribution.
d) If you travel abroad, it is important to observe the customs of the country you are visiting.
e) Are you still seeing Peter?
f) "That wasn't very smart," he observed.
g) The police observed the criminals from the house across the road.
h) As I see it, she's making a big mistake.

> to watch   to understand   to comment/remark   to admit
> to follow or obey a law/rule   to have an opinion on something
> to meet someone socially or date someone   to acknowledge

3 How would you translate *observe, recognize,* and *see* into your own language? Do the translations have multiple meanings?

4 Write a paragraph using *observe, recognize,* and *see*. Use each word once. Show it to a partner and ask him/her to figure out the meanings of the verbs you have used.

The Five Senses

1 Work with a partner and discuss these questions:

a) What are the five senses?
b) Which do you think is the most important to you in your everyday life?
c) Which would you be able to cope the best without?
d) Which sense triggers the most memories?
e) Have you ever lost the use of one of your senses temporarily?
f) Do you think any of your senses is especially well-developed?

2 30 Listen to Mike, Maria, Helen, Nick, and Petra each answering one of the questions in 1. Take notes on their answers. Which senses are they talking about? Which question is each person answering?

3 Compare your notes with your partner. Were the speakers' answers similar to yours?

Close-up

Verbs of the senses

Language Reference p. 58

1 Work with a partner. Look at the verbs in the box. Which refer to an ability? Which refer to an action? Which can refer to both?

smell   feel   see   look   hear   listen   taste   touch

2 Complete these excerpts from the speakers' answers, using the correct forms of the verbs in the box. You may need to add a modal auxiliary or a negative.

a) Yes, the most important one is sight, I guess… I mean, if you're blind, if you (1) _____ , then although you can lead a full life and all that, I think it does make you more vulnerable, more dependent on other people…

b) …I would really hate it if I (2) _____ what things or people looked like… or the expressions on people's faces when they're talking to you. I mean, you wouldn't even know if they (3) _____ at you or whether they looked interested in what you were saying.

c) …I read this article about a man who went deaf, and then his hearing was restored to him, and he spoke about how isolating it can be if you (4) _____ .

d) …he really missed (5) _____ to music; that was the worst part, he said. That and not being able to (6) _____ his wife's voice.

e) …I (7) _____ the palm trees, (8) _____ the food, (9) _____ the sun on my skin…

f) …they used an international sign language that was based on touch; they would (10) _____ each other and sign on each other's palms, and they (11) _____ each other talking—and it showed them going to a drum concert, too—like a traditional Japanese drum concert—and they (12) _____ the music, I mean they (13) _____ the vibrations of the drums, even though they (14) _____ them.

g) …I'm really sensitive to things like gas leaks and anything that (15) _____ bad…

h) …I (16) _____ really strong things, like coffee or if something's burning in the kitchen, but I (17) _____ other things like perfume, so I don't know how much to put on. And I really miss the subtler smells in the kitchen. It affects my taste, too. Everything (18) _____ so bland.

3 🔊 31 Listen and check your answers.

4 Were your answers different from the speakers' answers? If yes, do you think your answers are also correct?

5 Look at the verbs in *italics* in the following sentences. Which describe:
- an ability or a sensation?
- an action?

a) He's amazing; he can *hear* a tune just once and then reproduce it perfectly.
b) When *I'm watching* a movie at the movie theater, I like to sit in the middle of a row so that I can *see* more clearly.
c) When you have a bad cold, you can't really *taste* things well.
d) When it's windy, you can't always *feel* how hot the sun is on your skin, so it's very easy to get sunburned.
e) "Don't *touch* that plate—it just came out of the oven."
f) The teacher got really angry because none of the children *were listening* to what he was saying.
g) It was a terrible fire; they could *feel* the hot air and *smell* the smoke a mile away.
h) Always *smell* wine before *tasting* it.
i) If you turn the volume down a little, you'll be able to *hear* it much more clearly.
j) He *didn't look* before crossing the street and was almost hit by a bus!

6 Look at the sentences again and discuss these questions with your partner:

a) Which verbs are used to describe an ability or a sensation?
b) Which verbs are used to describe an action?
c) Find the modal auxiliaries and any other phrases with similar meanings. Are they used with descriptions of ability, descriptions of action, or both?

Mind UNIT 6 57

7 Complete each sentence with the correct form of an appropriate verb from 6 on page 57.
   a) Sometimes I found it difficult to concentrate in class. I used to tune out and ____ out the window, and I ____ to a word the teacher said.
   b) Sometimes groupwork can be really difficult. I just ____ what people are saying when there are a lot of people talking at the same time.
   c) If I were nearsighted, I'd have laser treatment on my eyes so that I ____ without having to wear glasses.
   d) I find that I can remember a word much better if I ____ it written down.
   e) When I ____ freshly cut grass, I always think of my dad and his lawn mower in the summer.
   f) When I was a kid, I hated cabbage. I just couldn't eat it. If there was even the slightest trace of it, say in a soup or something, I ____ it right away and absolutely refused to eat it.
   g) I used to ____ perfectly when I was younger, but now I need to wear glasses when I read or go to the movies.
   h) I love summer evenings when you can sit outside, and you ____ the heat of the sun still on your skin.

8 Are any of these sentences true for you? Discuss each one with a partner.

9 Work with a partner. Look at the pairs of sentences below.
   a) Discuss the difference in meaning of the verbs in *italics* in each pair.
   b) Which verbs are stative and which are dynamic?

1A I *can see* John. He's just over there, standing next to the bookcase.
1B I'm *seeing* John tomorrow. I'll let him know what we've decided.

2A I *could hear* strange sounds coming from downstairs, so I decided to go and investigate.
2B I've been *hearing* great things about you recently. You must be doing really well.

3A I'm not *feeling* very well; I think I'm going to go and lie down for a while.
3B That heater's really good! I *can feel* the heat from here.

4A I'm just *tasting* the soup to see if I need to add any more salt.
4B I really *can't taste* the difference between butter and margarine.

5A She was in the garden *smelling* the roses when she was stung by a bee.
5B We lived near a chocolate factory. It was great. You *could smell* it all around you.

Verbs with **dynamic** meanings refer to action or change.
I **spent** the weekend in Miami. She's **gained** a lot of weight recently.

Verbs with **stative** meanings refer to a state or condition. They are usually not used in continuous forms or imperatives.
I **love** my husband. He **believes** that his method is right.

Language Reference: Verbs of the senses

We can talk about senses in two ways:
- using stative verbs, to refer to abilities or sensations
- using dynamic verbs, to refer to voluntary actions

Stative verbs	Dynamic verbs
see	look (at)/watch
feel	touch/feel
hear	listen (to)
smell	smell
taste	taste

can, could, and be able to

We can often use stative verbs with *can, could,* or *be able to.*

I **can see** much better when I'm wearing my glasses.
I **could smell** the smoke, but I **couldn't see** the fire.
I would love to **be able to hear** as well as I **could** when I was younger.

Continuous forms

We rarely use verbs with stative meanings in continuous forms. When they are used in continuous forms, the meanings usually change and they become dynamic.

I'm **seeing** the car over there. ✗
I'm **seeing** the doctor tomorrow about my back. ✓
(meaning = meeting)

I'm **feeling** your hand on my shoulder. ✗
I'm **feeling** much better today. ✓
(meaning = talking about your state of health)

I'm **smelling** gas. ✗
He's **smelling** her new perfume. ✓
(meaning = investigating)

I'm **tasting** too much salt in this dish. ✗
They're **tasting** the dessert to see if they like it. ✓
(meaning = testing)

I'm **hearing** beautiful music coming from the apartment upstairs. ✗
She's **been hearing** good reports about his work. ✓
(meaning = being told about something)

Pet Psychology

Discussion Work in small groups and discuss these questions:

a) Have you ever had a pet? What was it? What was its name?
b) What's the most unusual pet you've heard of? Why do you think people keep such animals?
c) Do you think pets serve a useful function? If so, what?
d) Do you think people get too attached to their pets?

Reading **1** Match the problems to the definitions.

a) nervous breakdown   1 hostile action taken toward trespassers
b) addiction   2 the condition of doing or consuming something habitually and being unable to give it up
c) separation anxiety   3 a loss of mental health and strength
d) phobia   4 a state of uneasiness brought about by the absence of a person or thing
e) territorial aggression 5 an irrational fear or hatred of something

2 Read this pet case history and decide which of the problems above Willy was suffering from.

The Canine Cruncher

The day Mr. X took delivery of his new van was the day his dog decided to start out on a new career. Previously a docile creature, Willy the cross-bred terrier turned into Lex Flex, the Canine Cruncher, in the time it took his owner to eat a three-course meal.

Having left his trusty companion to keep an eye on the sporty new van, Mr. X returned from lunch to find that his new mode of transportation had been completely remodeled. What had been a sturdy, dependable method of delivering frozen foods around downtown would now not have looked out of place by a beach on a hot summer's day. The roof had been torn back as if with a can opener, an air-conditioning system had been thoughtfully provided by the removal of the windshield, and the seats had been given a new look that might have been described as "ripped and tattered." Exhausted by all his hard work, Willy was taking a nap when his owner reappeared.

Speechless, Mr. X rushed toward his hound with his arms outstretched. Waking up with a start, Willy sat up to greet his owner and barked with excitement. However, being a modest sort of dog and not thinking it necessary for his devoted owner to thank him so profusely, he bounded through the shattered windshield and took off down the street. Mr. X's voice could be heard fading into the distance behind him as he raced away. Overcome with emotion, the van owner returned to survey the full extent of the new design.

These days it's not uncommon to see Mr. X driving around the streets of the city looking for his absent friend. Numbed by the efficiency of his new air-conditioning system, he's often spotted scouring the streets between deliveries, under the protection of a warm blanket. Rumor has it that he's going to send Willy away to a special dog camp when they are reunited, just as a small token of his appreciation.

3 Work with a partner and discuss the meanings of these expressions.

a) a docile creature (line 3)
b) ripped and tattered (lines 20–21)
c) a nap (line 22)
d) Rumor has it (lines 43)
e) a small token of his appreciation (lines 46)

4 The text contains a lot of descriptive language. However, the actual events of the story can be summarized in a few sentences. Write as short a factual account of the story as you can.

Close-up

Participial clauses

1 Without looking back, make three sentences from the text, using one clause from each column.

COLUMN 1	COLUMN 2	COLUMN 3
a) Having left his trusty companion	he's often spotted scouring the streets between deliveries,	and barked with excitement.
b) Waking up with a start,	to keep an eye on the sporty new van,	under the protection of a warm blanket.
c) Numbed by the efficiency of his new air-conditioning system,	Willy sat up to greet his owner	Mr. X returned from lunch to find that his new mode of transportation had been completely remodeled.

2 Look back at the text and check your answers.

Language Reference p. 61

3 Look at your answers to 1 and answer these questions:

a) Find the *participial clause* in each sentence. Which contains a
   • present participle?   • past participle?   • perfect participle?
b) What is the subject of each participial clause?
c) Where is the subject of each participial clause?

4 Look at this pair of sentences and answer the questions.

A Exhausted by all his hard work, Willy was taking a nap when…
B Willy was exhausted by all his hard work, so he was taking a nap when…

a) Which sentence, A or B, is more likely to be spoken? Which was used in the text? Look back and check.
b) What has been added to B to replace the participial clause?

5 Rewrite these sentences, using participial clauses.

a) When I graduated from college, I took a year off to travel and give myself time to decide what to do next.
b) After my last English exam, I went straight to bed because I was totally exhausted.
c) Because I live by myself, I don't really do a lot of cooking.
d) I have a large car, so I'm often the driver when I go out with friends.
e) I like to spend the weekends relaxing because I'm tired after a long week at work.

6 Are any of these sentences true for anyone in your class?

7 Work with a partner. Look at the following sentences and add *not* where necessary.

a) Wanting to offend people, they decided to extend the guest list to include both family and friends.
b) Discouraged by the long climb ahead of them, they set off at dawn, chatting happily.
c) Having completed the form, she sent it with a photograph to the address below.
d) Jean has a clear grasp of the grammar, but having spoken English in years, he lacks confidence in conversation.
e) Knowing that arriving on time would make a very bad impression, he left with plenty of time to spare.
f) Relieved at hearing that she had passed, Sandra immediately called her parents.

8 What do you notice about the position of *not* in the sentences in 7?

9 Rephrase your answers to 7 without using participial clauses. You may need to add linking words.

For example:
They didn't want to offend people, so they decided to extend the guest list to include both family and friends.

UNIT 6 *Mind*

Language Reference: Participial clauses

Participial clauses do not include a subject or linking words. You can form them with a:

Present participle
Being a little shy, he chose not to speak in front of everybody.
Not having a lot of time, they decided to take a taxi.
In these cases, the participle is substituting for the subject and a different form of the verb:
Because he was a little shy, he chose not to speak in front of everybody.
Because they didn't have a lot of time, they decided to take a taxi.

Past participle
Woken by a noise, James called the police.
Not taken in by his charm, she refused his offer of dinner.
In these cases, the participle is substituting for the subject and the verb *be*:
James was woken by a noise, so he called the police.

She wasn't taken in by his charm, so she refused his offer of dinner.

Perfect participle
Not having understood the question, she failed to answer it correctly.
Having mixed the chemicals together, we observed the reaction.
In these cases, the perfect participle is substituting for the subject and a verb in the past perfect.
Because she hadn't understood the question, she failed to answer it correctly.
After we had mixed the chemicals together, we observed the reaction.

Note: Participial clauses are often used to avoid repetition and to shorten complex sentences. They are more commonly found in written language, such as narratives, reports, and essays.

Mind

Expressions with *mind*

1 Look at the expression in **bold** in each sentence. Is *mind* a verb or a noun in each one?

a) Oh, **don't mind me**; I'll be fine here by myself.
b) They pay really well. **Mind you**, they can afford it.
c) Don't worry, we'll figure it out somehow. **Something will come to mind**.
d) Jen invited me to go on vacation with her, but **I'm of two minds about it**.
e) What annoys me about him is the fact that he keeps **changing his mind** all the time.
f) Stop wasting time; **make up your mind!**
g) **Never mind!** I'm sure you'll do much better next time.
h) **Do you mind** if I open the window?
i) Don't worry about what other people think; just **speak your mind!**
j) **Bear in mind** that you're not as young as you used to be!

2 Match each expression in 1 with one of these meanings.

1 Say what you honestly think
2 On the other hand
3 You'll think of an idea
4 Don't worry
5 I can't decide
6 Would it bother you
7 Don't forget
8 Don't worry about
9 Altering his opinion
10 Make a decision

3 Do you know any other expressions with *mind*?

4 Work with a partner. Discuss these questions:

a) When was the last time you were of two minds about something?
b) Do you mind if people smoke in restaurants?
c) When was the last time you spoke your mind? Did you offend anyone?

Word linking

1 ▶ 32 Listen to a conversation among three people. Where are they? Who do you think the boss is? Why?

2 Look at these sentences from the conversation. Complete them with expressions including *mind*.

> a) Listen, John, ____ leaving the room for a minute? There's something I need to discuss with Pete.
> b) Uh-oh. I think I know what you're going to say. ____ if I smoke?
> c) I guess I'm not that surprised. That's what we get for ____ to the client, right?

3 Listen again and check your answers.

4 Look at the following phrases. How do the speakers pronounce the underlined sections? Practice saying the phrases.

Woul<u>d you</u> mind   <u>Do you</u> mind

5 Work with a partner and discuss the following questions. Think carefully about the pronunciation of the underlined sections.

   a) <u>Did you</u> do anything special last night?
   b) <u>Do you</u> prefer tea or coffee?
   c) <u>Do you</u> mind if people keep you waiting?
   d) Woul<u>d you</u> mind if someone borrowed something of yours without asking?
   e) <u>Did you</u> go anywhere on vacation last year?
   f) What woul<u>d you</u> do if you won a lot of money in the lottery?
   g) <u>Do you</u> go to the movies a lot, or <u>do you</u> prefer to rent videos?
   h) How woul<u>d you</u> react if your parents told you they were going to live abroad?

I'm Going Slightly Mad

1 Look at the pictures. There's something going wrong in each one. What is it?

2 ▶ 33 Listen to the song. All the images in the pictures are included. Note the order in which they are mentioned.

3 Listen again. What other images and metaphors are used to describe the singer's state of mind? Look at tapescript 33 on page A84 if you need help.

4 What do you know about Freddie Mercury? Why do you think he wrote this song?

Queen

Freddie Mercury, Roger Taylor, Brian May, and John Deacon formed the rock group **Queen** in the early 1970s. They released their first album, **Queen,** in 1973 and soon gained a reputation for their flamboyancy. They recorded the album *Innuendo,* on which *I'm Going Slightly Mad* appears, in 1990, shortly before Mercury died in 1991.

62   UNIT 6 *Mind*

7 Review 1

NEWS IN BRIEF

Counting on the Money
A woman, (1) *obsessed* with Dracula and vampires since she was a child, has set up a company (2) *importing* coffins from Transylvania.

High and Dry
Emergency staff at a hospital treated a man last week after he inhaled fumes from his socks, (3) ____ while drying in front of an electric heater.

Stolen Moments
Women (4) ____ french fries from their partners' plates are the most common cause of arguments between couples (5) ____, according to a recent poll.

Crisis Point
The guest speaker at a meeting in Plymouth last night had to abandon his talk, (6) ____ "How to Cope in a Crisis," when he was called home because his house was on fire.

Compact Case
A Midlands police force is seeking a make-up artist to make volunteers (7) ____ in police lineups look more like the suspected criminals.

Whole in One
A man (8) ____ his wife to a bingo game in order to stop her from complaining about the amount of golf he plays won $300,000!

Flower Power
A florist is offering bunches of dead roses (9) ____ in black paper for jilted lovers to send to their former partners.

Deeply in Love
A couple (10) ____ while learning to scuba dive got married in a tank full of tropical fish.

Relative and participial clauses

1 The stories above are all taken from newspapers. Complete each relative or participial clause by adding a verb from the box in the correct form. You may also need to add a relative pronoun. The first two have been done for you.

> ~~import~~   catch fire   entitle   eat out   steal   take part
> ~~obsess~~   wrap   accompany   meet

2 One of the stories is not true. Which one is it? Check your answer on page A68.

Verb forms Complete the newspaper story by putting the verbs in parentheses into the correct form.

SNAKES ALIVE!

A young groom-to-be with a phobia of snakes (1) *woke* (wake) up on the morning of his wedding (2) ____ (find) his room and his body covered in snakes about 12 inches long. Mike Sanders, 22, who (3) ____ (marry) at 2 o'clock that afternoon, was so terrified that he (4) ____ (can/not/move) or even (5) ____ (call) for help, (6) ____ (believe) the slightest twitch (7) ____ (result) in his immediate death. (8) ____ (lie) in his bed, and despite the frantic knocking of his bride on the door, he (9) ____ (remain) motionless as the hour of his wedding (10) ____ (come) and (11) ____ (go). He (12) ____ (eventually/rescue) when police officers (13) ____ (break into) his house. The story (14) ____ (come) out that the snakes were plastic, certainly not poisonous, and (15) ____ (put) there by friends as a joke after the bachelor party.

Clearly shaken a week later and still (16) ____ (not/speak) to his friends since his ordeal, Mr. Sanders (17) ____ (tell) reporters, "Snakes (18) ____ (always/be) my biggest fear ever since I was a child. My so-called friends were well aware that I (19) ____ (not/find) it in the slightest bit funny. I (20) ____ (not/think) I (21) ____ (ever/be able) (22) ____ (forgive) them."

(23) ____ it ____ (not/be) for his friends' misplaced sense of fun, Mr. and Mrs. Sanders (24) ____ (today/celebrate) one week as husband and wife.

Words of Wisdom

Negative and limiting adverbials

1 Join the two parts of each of these famous quotes. The first one has been done for you.

1 Time is like a river made up of events. No sooner does anything appear
2 Not until it is too late
3 Only when I am unbearably unhappy
4 Not only should justice be done,
5 Never before have we had so little time
6 Not only is the universe queerer than we suppose,
7 Never has a man turned so little knowledge
8 Not only did he not suffer fools gladly,

a) to such great account.
b) do I have the true feeling of myself.
c) does one recognize the really important moments in one's life.
d) to do so much.
e) than it is swept away and something else comes into its place.
f) but it should manifestly and undoubtedly be seen to be done.
g) he did not suffer them at all.
h) but queerer than we *can* suppose.

2 Match the quotes with the people below. Check your answers on page A70.

a) Roman Emperor Marcus Aurelius Antoninus philosophizing about change. *Quote 1*
b) U.S. President Franklin D. Roosevelt in a speech to Congress in 1941
c) Former Lord Chief Justice of the United Kingdom, Gordon Hewitt
d) British geneticist J. B. S. Haldane contemplating extraterrestrial life
e) Anonymous: about U.S. Statesman Dean Acheson
f) Dramatist and poet T. S. Elliot talking about Shakespeare
g) Crime writer Agatha Christie reflecting on her life
h) Czech novelist Franz Kafka baring his soul

3 Are there any other well-known words of wisdom or famous quotes that you like?

Discussion Bingo

1 You are going to play a game of bingo. Follow the rules below.

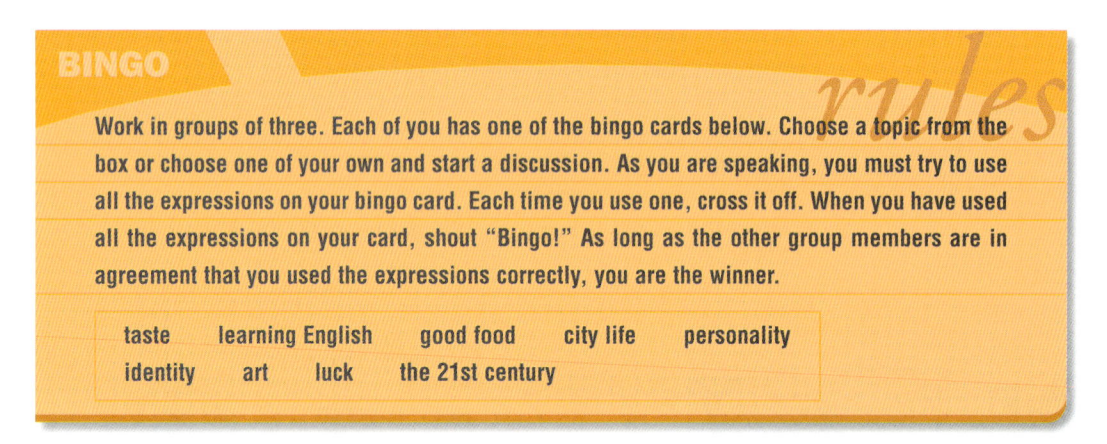

BINGO rules

Work in groups of three. Each of you has one of the bingo cards below. Choose a topic from the box or choose one of your own and start a discussion. As you are speaking, you must try to use all the expressions on your bingo card. Each time you use one, cross it off. When you have used all the expressions on your card, shout "Bingo!" As long as the other group members are in agreement that you used the expressions correctly, you are the winner.

| taste | learning English | good food | city life | personality |
| identity | art | luck | the 21st century | |

CARD 1
Speaking of…
It seems that…
When I was younger, I'd often…
Not necessarily, because…
I really regret…
Oh, come on…

CARD 2
Frankly, …
Gone are the times…
I really wish…
There is no doubt that…
People will always…
Only when…

CARD 3
Actually, …
It's not known whether…
If only…
You should bear in mind…
I tend to…
On the whole, …

2 Choose a different card and a different topic and play again.

All Change

Position of adverbials

1 Work with a partner and read each pair of sentences. Explain the difference in meaning between them.

a) A I don't really want to go.
   B I really don't want to go.
b) A I think John has only his phone number.
   B I think only John has his phone number.
c) A I'm a hundred percent certain she's not going.
   B I'm not a hundred percent certain she's going.
d) A I did my work quickly and got ready to go out.
   B I did my work and quickly got ready to go out.
e) A I really like your T-shirt.
   B I like your T-shirt, really.
f) A I never knew you'd been there.
   B I knew you'd never been there.
g) A Personally, I don't think he'll apologize.
   B I don't think he'll apologize personally.
h) A For a moment, I didn't believe him.
   B I didn't believe him for a moment.
i) A I'm sure he'll still be here in the morning.
   B I'm still sure he'll be here in the morning.
j) A Just Sam and I went for a drink.
   B Sam and I just went for a drink.

Ian, John, Helena, and Angela

2 34 Listen to ten short dialogues that correspond to the pairs of sentences in 1. Is the second speaker's comment closer in meaning to sentence A or B in each dialogue?

3 Work with a partner. Write some similar dialogues and sentences of your own.

4 Work in small groups and read your dialogues and sentences. Ask the other members of your group to guess which of the two sentences is closer in meaning to the dialogue.

Ready, Set, Go!

Phrasal verbs

1 Find nine more phrasal verbs in the grid below. The verbs go →, ↓ and ↘.

T	L	O	O	K	I	N	T	O	H	R	S
R	H	X	B	O	T	T	L	E	U	P	Z
G	A	I	B	R	E	A	K	O	F	F	C
U	E	S	N	V	B	L	Q	O	J	G	O
T	S	T	E	K	R	K	N	M	B	E	M
O	P	L	A	C	T	F	Y	E	R	T	E
L	I	E	W	C	H	H	G	Z	I	D	U
W	C	G	D	T	R	R	R	N	N	O	P
X	K	A	U	L	O	O	P	O	G	W	W
H	U	W	I	F	H	V	S	K	U	N	I
T	P	K	J	Z	A	G	T	S	P	G	T
T	F	L	I	P	T	H	R	O	U	G	H

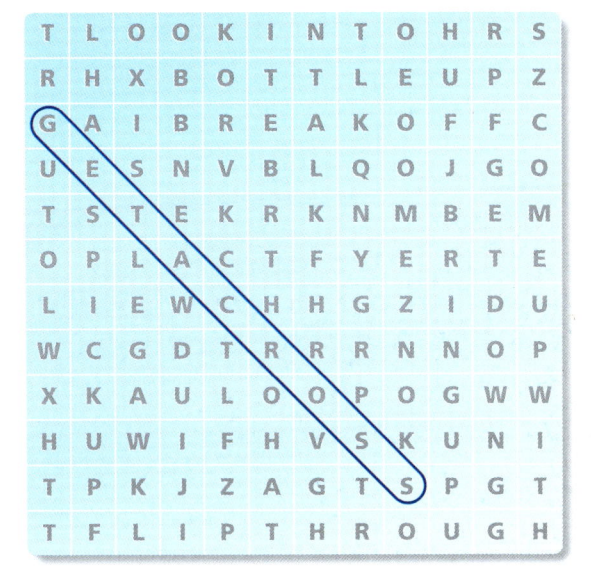

2 Choose four of the verbs and write three sentences for each one. Trade sentences with other students in the class until you have one for each verb.

Review 1 UNIT 7 65

Greetings from Down Under

General review

1 Read Juliette's e-mail to her friends and correct her mistakes. There are at least twenty mistakes.

From: Juliette <juliette@kanga.com>
Subject: Australia
▷ Attachments: Picture of Sydney Harbor

Dear all,

Since it was so long since I've written, I thought it was time I dropped all you a line or two from not-so-sunny Australia! The weather has gotten really awful here unfortunately in Sydney over the last few days. I think summer is finally over! Never mind it, it'll give me the chance to do all the things I've been putting off while I've been lying on the beach taking it easy!

Life here is great—I've just found a job which is working in a café little and friendly near the harbor. Actually, Lena, it's the place recommended your friend. It only is a few hours each week, but the pay is good, and there are working there some great people. The most of them are also traveling around the world like me. In fact, a few days ago I met someone thinking he met you all in Vietnam. Do you remember an English guy called Kim? He says it was somewhere in the mountains—he told me the name, but I can't remember it.

Anyway, I'm here in Australia for almost a month now. As you know, Marcella decided to for a while stay in Thailand with Yuichi. They seem totally in love! He is really nice. I'm sure Marcella has told you all about it by now! Anyway, I was really glad to stop moving after all the buses, trains, and planes I was taking to get here from Bangkok. Well, I say "moving"! Often the buses would stop in some remote town or village for what was feeling like hours! Nobody got off the bus in case it suddenly left without them. At the time I wished I flew here, but looking back, it was an experience! Consequently, I spent when I first arrived a few days relaxing and wandering around the city, and then I went on a trip along the coast for a couple of weeks before going to the Blue Mountains for few days. The mountains, which aren't that far from Sydney, absolutely are incredible—very beautiful and peaceful.

So, what about all of you? You must e-mail me back and let me know all the gossip back home. Miguel and Virginia, how's the new house? And how are you two, Lena and Stefan? By the way, are you hearing the new Superhead CD yet? If not, you should check out it—it's amazing! You first met at their concert, didn't you?

Well, I'll finish now—I have to go work at the café. I miss you all lots—if only you are all here with me. Now that I've stopped traveling around for a while, I'll write more often—I promise! Hope you like the picture! Write back soon.

Lots of love,

Juliette xxxxxx

---

2 Write a letter or an e-mail to a friend, telling him/her your news.

66 UNIT 7 Review 1

The Word Game

Vocabulary

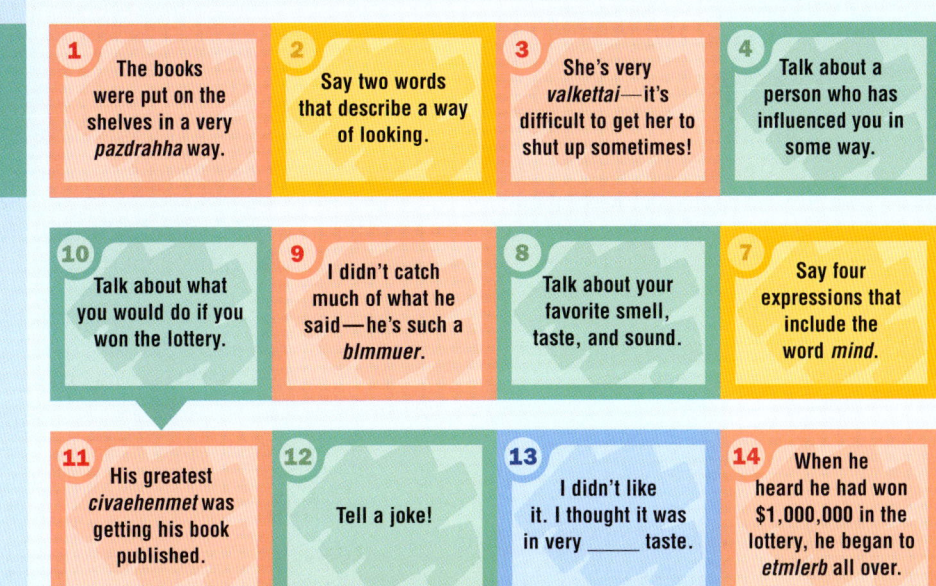

START

1. The books were put on the shelves in a very *pazdrahha* way.
2. Say two words that describe a way of looking.
3. She's very *valkettai*—it's difficult to get her to shut up sometimes!
4. Talk about a person who has influenced you in some way.
5. We went to a really *lzgiyt* restaurant on my birthday.

10. Talk about what you would do if you won the lottery.
9. I didn't catch much of what he said—he's such a *blmmuer*.
8. Talk about your favorite smell, taste, and sound.
7. Say four expressions that include the word *mind*.
6. I couldn't get a word in ____! He just went on and on and…

11. His greatest *civaehenmet* was getting his book published.
12. Tell a joke!
13. I didn't like it. I thought it was in very ____ taste.
14. When he heard he had won $1,000,000 in the lottery, he began to *etmlerb* all over.
15. Say three words made from the word *taste*.

20. They were having a very in-____ discussion about politics or something.
19. I don't think he *nedcgroiez* how important it was.
18. Talk about an early memory.
17. Her sister has wonderful taste ____ furniture.
16. The boys stole a car and went for a ____ before crashing it.

21. Say three words that can describe a discussion or conversation.
22. The streets were ____ with traffic, which made it difficult to travel around the city.
23. We've discovered a new restaurant with an *eiieuxqst* menu.
24. I didn't think they ____ their ideas across very well.
25. Talk about your favorite restaurant

30. The mountain range was really *ewa-gsniprini*.
29. Talk about your favorite city.
28. Have you heard about Jane's ____ to chocolate? She can't get enough of it!
27. Say an informal word that means *steal*.
26. *Romur* has it that the two companies are going to merge.

31. How about lunch? Please ____ in Friday at noon.
32. Tell about something you regret.
33. That's a *yczra* idea!
34. Talk about your hometown.
35. It's never a good idea to ____ up your feelings.

FINISH

RULES

Play in small groups. You will need a die and counters. The first player rolls the die and moves along the board from the Start, according to the number on the die. The player completes the task on the square he/she lands on. If the player is successful, he/she can play in the next round. If not, he/she misses the next turn. The winner is the first player to reach the Finish.

There are four types of tasks:

- Unscramble a mixed-up word.
- Add a missing word.
- Find words or expressions.
- Talk about something for thirty seconds without stopping.

Review 1 UNIT 7 67

Additional material

1 Identity
Introduction, 2
Answers
a) Denzel Washington
b) Marilyn Monroe
c) Penelope Cruz
d) George W. Bush

1 Identity
Mistaken Identity, 6
Answers
a) The man has just put his children to bed and is creeping back downstairs so he doesn't wake them up.
b) The woman has just bought a CD as a birthday present for her friend. She was taking the CD out of the shopping bag to look at it again when she saw the friend walk into the store.
c) The man on the left has noticed that something is about to fall from the building site. He's about to push the businessman out of the way so he doesn't get hurt.

1 Identity
The Gender Gap, 3
Student A

1. Make notes on the following:
   a) What Martians value
   b) How they experience fulfillment
   c) How their clothes reflect their value system
   d) What they are interested in
   e) What they take pride in
   f) What most annoys them

LIFE ON MARS

Martians value power, competency, efficiency, and achievement. They are always doing things to prove themselves and develop their power and skills. Their sense of self is defined through their ability to achieve results. They experience fulfilment primarily through success and accomplishment.

A man's sense of self is defined through his ability to achieve results.

Everything on Mars is a reflection of these values. Even their dress is designed to reflect their skills and competence. Police officers, soldiers, businessmen, scientists, cab drivers, technicians, and chefs all wear uniforms or at least hats to reflect their competence and power.

They don't read magazines like *Psychology Today*, *Self*, or *People*. They are more concerned with outdoor activities, like hunting, fishing, and racing cars. They are interested in the news, weather, and sports and couldn't care less about romance novels and self-help books.

They are more interested in 'objects' and 'things' rather than people and feelings. Even today on Earth, while women fantasize about romance, men fantasize about powerful cars, faster computers, gadgets, gizmos, and new powerful technology. Men are preoccupied with the 'things' that can help them express power by creating results and achieving their goals.

Achieving goals is very important to a Martian because it is a way for him to prove his competence and thus feel good about himself. And for him to feel good about himself he must achieve these goals by himself. Someone else can't achieve them for him. Martians pride themselves in doing things all by themselves. Autonomy is a symbol of efficiency, power and competence.

Understanding this Martian characteristic can help women understand why men resist so much being corrected or being told what to do. To offer a man unsolicited advice is to presume that he doesn't know what to do or that he can't do it on his own. Men are very touchy about this, because the issue of competence is so very important to them.

Because he is handling his problems on his own, a Martian rarely talks about his problems unless he needs expert advice. He reasons: 'Why involve someone else when I can do it by myself?' He keeps his problems to himself unless he requires help from another to find a solution. Asking for help when you can do it yourself is perceived as a sign of weakness.

(From *Men Are From Mars, Women Are From Venus*, by John Gray, Ph.D.)

2. When you have finished, turn back to page 8.

2 Taste
Introduction, 2
Answers
a) baked beans: Nicholas
b) cauliflower: Melody
c) a bar of chocolate: Rita
d) nuts: David

3 City
Where in the World?, 2
Clue 1

The text describes five cities from the list below:

Bangkok, Budapest, London, Madrid, Moscow, New York, Paris, Rio de Janeiro, Rome, Tokyo

Look at page A73 if you need another clue.

5 Luck
Winning the Big One. Vocabulary, 2
Answers

(1) c (2) b (3) b (4) a
(5) a (6) b (7) c (8) a

7 Review 1
Relative and participial clauses, 2
Answer

Deeply in Love. The tank was full of sharks, not tropical fish!

A68 ADDITIONAL MATERIAL

1 Identity

My Girl, 5

Student A

> Last night you and your boyfriend decided to go see a movie you both really want to see. Tonight is the last night it's showing. He's already canceled two dates to go. You're not too sure about your relationship right now. Your boyfriend seems to be very distant these days. You think there must be something worrying him, but he refuses to talk about it. You wish he'd talk to you, because you're sure it would help.

You call your boyfriend to make arrangements to meet. Think about what you're going to say and the language you are going to use.

3 City

One Big Party, 5

Student A

1 Below are four words from the text. Check their meanings in a dictionary if necessary and prepare to explain the words to your partner. Do not tell your partner the word you are explaining. Your partner must listen and identify the word from the text.
   a) renowned
   b) check out
   c) exorbitant
   d) rebound

2 When you have finished, listen to your partner's description of four more words from the text and identify the words being described.

4 Talk

Joke Time, 3

1 Before telling the story, it's important to identify the main stresses. Before you listen to the story again, look at the tapescript below and decide where the speaker pauses and where the main stresses fall. The first ones have been marked for you.

A <u>wealthy</u> woman returned home from a ball. //
She rang the bell for her butler, and when he appeared, she said, "Edward, take off my shoes," and he did. Then she said, "Edward, take off my coat," and he did. "Take off my dress," and he did. "And now, Edward," she said, "if you want to remain in my employment, you are never to wear any of my clothes again."

3 City

Hedging, 9

Many Young People Would Prefer to Live in Cities

According to a recent survey, it would appear that most people under the age of thirty would much prefer to live in large cities if given the choice.

By far, the most important factor given in their answers would seem to be the fact that it is much easier to find work in larger cities.

However, the results show that there is no doubt that the variety of recreational facilities available is also an important factor in the decision to leave families and homes in the suburbs.

6 Mind

Introduction, 2

Answers

a) False: the average male brain weighs 3.1 pounds and the average female brain weighs 2.9 pounds.
b) True
c) False: 80% of the average human brain is water.
d) False: the brain is pinkish gray on the surface and white inside.
e) True
f) False: we use 100% of our brains in everyday life.
g) True
h) False: the brain is very active during sleep, but the activity is different from waking activity.
i) False: we yawn more when the brain is being stimulated to allow more oxygen to the brain.
j) True

2 Compare your answers with a partner.

3 🎧 25 Listen again and check your answers. Make sure you note any differences.

4 Prepare to read the joke at the same time as it plays on the tape, mirroring the pauses and intonation. Follow the instructions below:

   a) Listen to the tape again. Read the tapescript quietly to yourself, trying to keep up with the tape as closely as possible.
   b) Read the story aloud the same way. Listen again and tell the joke aloud with the comedian.

1 Identity

The Gender Gap, 3

Student B

1. Take notes on the following:
   a) What Venusians value
   b) How they experience fulfillment
   c) How their dress reflects their value system
   d) What they are interested in and concerned with
   e) What they take pride in

LIFE ON VENUS

Venusians have different values. They value love, communication, beauty, and relationships. They spend a lot of time supporting, helping, and nurturing one another. Their sense of self is defined through their feelings and the quality of their relationships. They experience fulfilment through sharing and relating.

A woman's sense of self is defined through her feelings and the quality of her relationships.

5 Everything on Venus reflects these values. Rather than building highways and tall buildings, the Venusians are more concerned with living in harmony, community, and loving cooperation. Relationships are more important than work and technology. In most ways their world is the opposite of Mars.

They do not wear uniforms like Martians (to reveal their competence). On the
10 contrary, they enjoy wearing a different outfit every day, according to how they are feeling. Personal expression, especially of feelings, is very important. They may even change outfits several times a day as their mood changes.

Communication is of primary importance. To share their personal feelings is much more important than achieving goals and success. Talking and relating to
15 one another is a source of tremendous fulfilment.

This is hard for a man to comprehend. He can come close to understanding a woman's experience of sharing and relating by comparing it to the satisfaction he feels when he wins a race, achieves a goal, or solves a problem.

Instead of being goal oriented, women are relationship oriented; they are more
20 concerned with expressing their goodness, love, and caring. Two Martians go to lunch to discuss a project or business goal; they have a problem to solve. In addition, Martians view going to a restaurant as an efficient way to approach food: no shopping, no cooking, and no washing dishes. For Venusians, going to lunch is an opportunity to nurture a relationship, for both giving support to and receiving
25 support from a friend. Women's restaurant talk can be very open and intimate, almost like the dialogue that occurs between therapist and patient.

On Venus, everyone studies psychology and has at least a master's degree in counseling. They are very involved in personal growth, spirituality, and everything that can nurture life, healing, and growth. Venus is covered with parks,
30 organic gardens, shopping centers and restaurants.

Venusians are very intuitive. They have developed this ability through centuries of anticipating the needs of others. They pride themselves in being considerate of the needs and feelings of others. A sign of great love is to offer help and assistance to another Venusian without being asked.

(From *Men Are From Mars, Women Are From Venus*, by John Gray, Ph.D.)

2. When you have finished, turn back to page 8.

6 Mind

Mind matters, 3h

The Lost Mariner

The Lost Mariner is about a man suffering from amnesia. He could remember his childhood and the first years of his working life (he worked for the American navy) in great detail but nothing else. His world had stopped in 1945; he believed that he was a young man in his twenties, that America had won the war, and that Truman was the President of the U.S. He was unable to remember anything that had happened to him since.

The Phantom Finger

A sailor accidentally cut off his right index finger. For forty years afterward he was plagued by the phantom of the finger rigidly extended: whenever he scratched his nose or tried to eat, he was afraid that the phantom finger would poke his eye out. He knew that it was impossible, but the feeling was so strong he couldn't ignore it.

The Dog Beneath the Skin

This case concerns a young man who dreamed he was a dog and could smell like a dog. He then woke up and found he was indeed able to smell like a dog. He could distinguish all his friends by smell; he could smell their emotions — fear, contentment, worry — like a dog. It was a whole new world, but then suddenly, after three weeks, this strange transformation ceased.

7 Review 1

Words of wisdom, 2

Answers

Quote 1: Marcus Aurelius Antoninus
Quote 2: Agatha Christie
Quote 3: Franz Kafka
Quote 4: Gordon Hewitt
Quote 5: Franklin D. Roosevelt
Quote 6: J. B. S. Haldane
Quote 7: T. S. Elliot
Quote 8: Anonymous, about Dean Acheson

1 Identity

My Girl, 5

Student B

> You and your girlfriend had talked about going to see a movie tonight, but you've had a hard day and you just want to have a quiet night home alone. You're not really excited about seeing the movie anyway, and you know your girlfriend's sister would love to see it. Maybe the two of them could go together. You and your girlfriend can go out another time when you're feeling more social. You know you wouldn't be good company tonight.

You know your girlfriend will be calling you soon. Think about what you're going to say to her and the language you're going to use.

2 Taste

The Demise of a Great Little Restaurant, 4

Student A

1 Read the text and make notes about the changes that have taken place:
   a) in the area surrounding the bar.
   b) in the bar on the jetty.
   c) to the boat and the boat ride to the island.

5

My wife had heard all about Le Palmier and was looking forward to our visit as much as I was. Driving to the jetty, we were surprised to find that what had once been a tiny
10 village was now a thriving tourist town. As I parked the car, I looked across the water to the island, where I saw a brand new sign with the restaurant's name in lights. We set off for Dominique's bar in the hope of finding her still serving exquisite wine from a barrel.
15 It was not to be. At the edge of the water stood a large bar with tables inside and out. As I pushed open the door, pop music blared out at me. I made my way to the bar to find out about the possibility of getting a table that evening. The woman I spoke to looked familiar, and I
20 realized I was speaking to Dominique. As she looked at her list of reservations, I noticed that a number of bus tours were booked in. It all looked terribly efficient.
   We were in luck—there had been a late cancellation. We ordered a drink and settled down to wait for our turn on the launch. But while the wait was the same—about an hour—the surroundings were not. As we sat sipping our pricey beers, people came and went all around us. The bar clearly catered to more than the restaurant clientele, but the number of people who were looking expectantly out across the water worried me slightly. Eventually our names
25 were called, along with around twenty others. I wondered how we were all going to fit into the five-seater launch that I remembered from my earlier visit.
   But there was no small launch any more. Instead, I saw bobbing up and down at the end of the walkway a sleek
30 boat with plenty of seating and an enormous motor at the back. We were helped aboard by a well-dressed crew member. As the boat sped off toward the island, I glanced back toward our rented car and saw a crowd of teenagers gathered around it. I wondered whether the stereo would
35 still be there when we returned.
   The trip across the water was speedy and efficient. Gone was the opportunity to chat with Marianne and find out what Didier had caught that day. Instead we listened to more music.

3 City

One Big Party, 5

Student B

1 Below are four words from the text. Check their meanings in a dictionary if necessary and prepare to explain the words to your partner.
   a) resiliency
   b) glimpse
   c) economical
   d) eateries

2 Your partner will explain four more words from the text. You must listen and identify the words being described. When your partner has finished, explain your four words for your partner to identify.

2 Compare your answers with another Student A.

3 Work with a different partner who read part B. Close your book and use your notes to tell your partner about the changes to the bar and the boat ride. Your partner will give you information about the changes to the restaurant.

4 Discuss whether your predictions about the changes were correct.

1 Identity

Mistaken Identity, 2

Answers

a) True
b) Unknown: The text doesn't tell us if he parked it or not.
c) True
d) Unknown: We don't know if the driver and the owner are the same person.
e) Unknown: We don't know who drove it away or why.
f) Unknown: We don't know if the police officer came because he/she was called, just happened to be passing by, or maybe saw on a security camera what was happening.
g) Unknown: We don't know whether the police officer was a man or a woman.
h) Unknown: In addition to the man who appeared and the police officer, we don't know if the driver and the owner are two different people or the same person.

2 Taste

A Taste for Travel, 3

Answers

Anne: Thailand   Bill: Hungary   Kim: Southern India   Steve: Spain

4 Talk

Conversation piece, 2

Definition 1

conversation *n.* **1** the informal exchange of ideas, information, etc. by spoken words. **2** an instance of this. [Middle English via Old French from Latin *conversatio -onis* (as CONVERSE¹)]

conversational *adj.* **1** of or in conversation. **2** fond of or good at conversation. **3** colloquial.
　conversationally *adv.*

conversationalist *n.* a person who is good at or fond of conversing.

conversation piece *n.* **1** a small genre painting of a group of figures. **2** a thing that serves as a topic of conversation because of its unusualness, etc.

Definition 2

conversation noun ★★★

❶ [C] a talk between two or more people, usually a private and informal one: *Later in the evening, the conversation turned to politics.* ✦ **+ with/between** *a conversation with my neighbor/between two friends* ✦ **have a conversation** *She had a long telephone conversation with her mother.*

❷ [U] informal talk between people: *With so much loud music, conversation was almost impossible.* ✦ **topic/subject of conversation** *He's so boring—his only topic of conversation is football.* ✦ **snatches of conversation** (=short parts of a conversation) *I overheard a few snatches of conversation and realized we were in trouble.*

get into conversation (with sb) to start talking to someone you have never met before: *She met Harry at the airport and they got into conversation.*

make conversation to talk to someone that you do not know well, in order to be polite, not because you really want to talk to them. This type of conversation is also called **small talk**: *"It's a nice party, isn't it?" I said, trying to make conversation.*

conversational adj ❶ a conversational style of writing or speaking is informal, like a private conversation: *She spoke in a quiet conversational tone.* ❷ relating to conversations: *conversational skills*—**conversationally** adv

conversationalist noun [C] someone who enjoys conversations and always has interesting or funny things to say

conversation piece noun [C] an interesting or unusual object that attracts attention and makes people start talking about it

(From *Macmillan English Dictionary, for Advanced Learners of American English*, published by Macmillan Publishers Ltd, 2001; © Bloomsbury Publishing Plc 2001.)

2 Taste

The Demise of a Great Little Restaurant, 4

Student B

1. Read the text and make notes about the changes that had taken place:
   a) in the seating area and the kitchen.
   b) to the menu.
   c) to the vegetable gardens.

2. Compare your answers with another Student B.

3. Work with your orginal partner who read part A. Close your book and use your notes to tell your partner about the changes to the restaurant. Your partner will give you information about the changes to the bar and the boat ride.

4. Discuss whether your predictions about the changes were correct.

Arriving on the island that second time was a totally different experience. There was now a mass of tables on a huge concrete terrace exposed to the sun. Between the tables ran waiters, carrying trays of drinks and food. Our waiter spoke to us in English and thrust menus into our hands as soon as we sat down.

I looked through the windows into what had been a small and homey kitchen and saw four chefs sweating over huge stoves. There was no sign of Marianne or Didier, and I didn't recognize their son among the army of waiters. On the paper tablecloth was a basket, but the bread in it was not homemade. It was what you could buy in any supermarket on the mainland.

Looking at the menu, I realized that the motor boat was picking up more than just passengers: the greatly expanded menu offered dishes that could not have been created using ingredients just from the island. Worst of all, the squid was now served in batter and accompanied by french fries.

I asked the waiter what had become of Didier and Marianne. They had retired about five years earlier and sold the business to an entrepreneur from the capital. Only Dominique remained. She had married a local boy and was managing the bar on the jetty. The restaurant was obviously profitable. As we sat and ate an unremarkable meal, the boat came and went two or three times, bringing new customers and taking away those who had already eaten.

After dinner we wandered unnoticed around the back of the main building and looked out over what had been the gardens. There were now a number of small concrete buildings, some with lights shining from the windows. The new owner had obviously decided that there was money to be made from offering tourists more than just dinner. They could now come and spend the night, have breakfast in the morning, and then return to the mainland.

As we climbed aboard the boat, considerably poorer, I found myself thinking about Marianne and what she would think if she could see the place now. My reverie was broken as we chugged to a halt at the end of the jetty. I looked over to the car and wondered whether the stereo was still there.

3 City

Where in the World?, 2

Clue 2

Here are photos of the five cities, but not in the correct order.

Verb structures

Basic structures

ASPECT	VOICE	TENSES Present	TENSES Past	MODALS will (would, must…)
simple	active	He **writes** letters.	He **wrote** letters.	He **will write** letters.
	passive	Letters **are written**.	Letters **were written**.	Letters **will be written**.
continuous	active	He **is writing** letters.	He **was writing** letters.	He **will be writing** letters.
	passive	Letters **are being written**.	Letters **were being written**.	Letters **will be being written**.*
perfect	active	He **has written** letters.	He **had written** letters.	He **will have written** letters.
	passive	Letters **have been written**.	Letters **had been written**.	Letters **will have been** written.
perfect continuous	active	He **has been writing** letters.	He **had been writing** letters.	He **will have been writing** letters.

*Note: We usually do not say *be being* or *been being*. Therefore, the future continuous passive and the present/past continuous passives are rare. For the same reason, the perfect continuous passive is almost never used.

Phrasal verbs
See unit 1.

Type 1: not separable
She quickly **looked over** her notes before starting her speech.
He **got over** his divorce remarkably quickly.
Can you **look after** the kids while I go to the store?

Type 2: separable
He **picked** the children **up** at school.
He **picked up** the children at school.
He **picked** them **up** at school.

Type 3: two particles
I couldn't **put up with** it any longer.
She finally managed to **stand up to** her boss at the meeting.
I'm really **looking forward to** the party.

Unreal conditionals
See unit 5.

	If clause	Main clause
Present reference	If I **were/was** on vacation	I **wouldn't feel** so stressed out.
	If I **weren't/wasn't working**,	I**'d be feeling** a lot more relaxed.
Future reference	If I **weren't/wasn't going** away next week,	I**'d be** happy to come to the party on Saturday.
	If I **were/was staying** at home,	I**'d be coming** to the party on Saturday.
Past reference	If I **had had** a little more free time,	I **would have been** happy to go to the party.
	If I **hadn't been working**,	I **would have been doing** something else.

Notes:
Any of the *if* clauses can be used in combination with any of the main clauses.
The structure *If I were you* is frequently used to give advice.

Inversion
See units 3 and 5.

Not only **do we need** food and drink to stay alive, but we also need love and affection.
Little **did I suspect** that I would come to love his strange ways.
Barely **had I opened** the door when I heard a loud noise upstairs.
So surprised **were we** by his extreme reaction that we said nothing in reply.
Had I known you were going to be so late, I would have left without you.

Patterns with *wish*
See unit 5.

1

Fact	Wish
I **don't have** many opportunities to speak English.	I wish I **had** more opportunities to speak English.
Pete**'s traveling** a lot for work these days.	I wish Pete **weren't/wasn't traveling** so much.
I **didn't know** what I was doing.	I wish I**'d known** what I was doing.
I **was wasting** my time.	I wish I **hadn't been wasting** my time.
We**'re going to be working** hard next week.	I wish we **weren't going to be working** so hard.
I **can't go** to the party.	I wish I **could go** to the party.
The sun **isn't shining**.	I wish the sun **would shine**.

2
We wish **to inform** you that the building will be closed until five o'clock today.

Participle clauses
See unit 6.

Present participle clause	**Eating a plum**, I came across a maggot. **Having some time to myself**, I drove to the shore for a couple of days.
Past participle clause	**Built in 1998**, this is probably one of the best examples of modern architecture downtown. The police, **trained in crowd control**, had trouble holding back the angry mob.
Perfect participle clause	**Not having seen the news**, she hadn't heard about the earthquake. **Having finished the book**, he breathed a sigh of relief.

Verbs of the senses
See unit 6.

Ability/Sensation (stative verbs)	Voluntary action (dynamic verbs)
I **can see** for miles and miles.	**Look at** that ship on the horizon.
I **could feel** the wind in my hair as I walked along the cliff.	We **were just feeling** the material when the store clerk accused us of stealing.
I **can hear** the siren from the fire station near my house.	**Are you going to listen** to the news?
Can you smell something burning?	**Smell** this! I think it's gone bad.
He **could taste** the nuts as soon as he took the first bite.	**Would you taste** this for me? Does it need more salt?

Grammar glossary

```
                      modal                                    main
verb  adjective  conjunction  auxiliary  adverb  article  pronoun  verb
```
Learn these useful words and you can understand more about the language you are studying.
```
determiner   noun   pronoun   main        preposition  noun  auxiliary
                              verb                            verb
```

Adverbials can be words or phrases. They are used to give additional information about a verb or an adjective or to comment on a statement.
For example: I *usually* try to go swimming **twice a week**. *Frankly*, I think that was a **really awful** thing he did.

Backshift is when a verb moves "one tense back" in a conditional clause or reported statement.
For example: "I can't come." ➔ He said he *couldn't* come.

clause is a group of words containing a verb.
For example: *He said*   *that he'd be late.*
              main clause   subordinate clause

Combinations refer to words that frequently occur together.
For example: *Common sense   Take care.   Happy Birthday*

Discourse markers are words or phrases that indicate the relationship between ideas.
For example: *Frank is a really good manager of people,* **whereas** *Tom is better with figures.*

Dynamic/Stative. Verbs can have dynamic or stative meanings. Verbs with dynamic meanings refer to action or change.
For example: I *walked* to the store.   I *read* the book.   I *got* very excited.
Verbs with stative meanings refer to states or conditions. They are not usually used in continuous forms or imperatives.
For example: I *know* her very well.   I *believe* in miracles.

Expressions are groups of words that belong together where the words and word order never or rarely change.
For example: *black and white   That reminds me,* I must buy some toothpaste.   *How do you do?*

Hedging is a tactic used to avoid stating a fact too categorically.
For example: *It seems that* the president may have made a mistake.

Inversion is when the auxiliary verb is placed in front of the subject.
For example: *Do you come* here often?   *Are you* sure?   Never *have I heard* such nonsense.
So shocked *was I* by the news that I let out a cry.

Noun phrases can be simply pronouns or nouns. Complex noun phrases can also include determiners, some description before the noun, and some description after the noun. The description after the noun is often a reduced clause or a prepositional phrase.
For example: *A strong cup of coffee with a little cream* is great in the morning.

Objects usually come after the verb and show who or what is affected by the verb.
For example: She closed **the window**.   My neighbor hates **me**.   I made **a pot of coffee**.
Note: some verbs take a direct object (DO) and an indirect object (IO).
For example: She gave **him** (IO) **a kiss** (DO).   He sent **her** (IO) **some flowers** (DO).   I teach **students** (IO) **English** (DO).

Particles are the prepositions or adverbs that form part of a phrasal verb.
For example: give *away*   give *up on*

Participial clauses do not include a subject or linking words and are often used to avoid repetition and to shorten complex sentences.
For example: *Sweating from his long run*, he collapsed on the chair.   The new bridge, **built in 2001**, was the pride of the community.

Phrasal verb is the term that commonly refers to all multi-word verbs that consist of a verb + particle(s).
For example: *to pick up   to look through   to run over   to put up with*

Prepositional phrases are phrases which consist of a preposition followed by a noun phrase or clause.
For example: *in my opinion   through the window   since I left school*

Relative clauses can be either restrictive or non-restrictive. A restrictive relative clause is necessary to identify the person or thing being talked about in the main clause.
For example: The people *who live next door* have three kids.
A non-restrictive relative clause is not necessary for identification and just gives extra information.
For example: The Smiths, *who have three children*, live next door.
Relative clauses are usually introduced by relative pronouns *who, that,* or *which* or by relative adverbs *whose, when, where, why*.

Reverse word order is when a word or phrase that is not usually used in the initial position of a sentence is placed at the beginning to create emphasis.
For example: *Gone* are the long summer evenings when we could sit outside until late.

Stative. See **Dynamic.**

Subjects usually come before the verb and refer to the main person or thing you are talking about.
For example: *Money* doesn't grow on trees.   *My tailor* is rich.   *The biggest rock and roll group in the world* have started their world tour.

Phonetic symbols

VOWELS AND DIPHTHONGS

/ɪ/	big fish	/bɪg fɪʃ/
/i/	green beans	/grin binz/
/ʊ/	should look	/ʃʊd lʊk/
/u/	blue moon	/blu mun/
/ɛ/	ten hens	/tɛn hɛnz/
/ə/	about bananas	/əbaʊt bənænəz/
/æ/	fat cat	/fæt kæt/
/ʌ/	must come	/mʌst kʌm/
/ɑ/	hot spot	/hɒt spɒt/
/ɔ/	fall ball	/fɔl bɔl/
/ei/	face	/feis/
/ɔi/	boy	/bɔi/
/ou/	nose	/nouz/
/ai/	eye	/ai/
/aʊ/	mouth	/maʊθ/
/ɪr/	dear	/dɪr/
/ɑr/	bar	/bɑr/
/ər/	learn words	/lərn wərdz/
/ɛr/	hair care	/hɛr kɛr/
/ɔr/	four sports	/fɔr spɔrts/

CONSONANTS

/p/	pen	/pɛn/
/b/	bad	/bæd/
/t/	tea	/ti/
/d/	dog	/dɔg/
/tʃ/	church	/tʃərtʃ/
/dʒ/	jazz	/dʒæz/
/k/	cost	/kɔst/
/g/	girl	/gərl/
/f/	far	/fɑr/
/v/	voice	/vɔis/
/θ/	thin	/θɪn/
/ð/	then	/ðɛn/
/s/	snake	/sneik/
/z/	noise	/nɔɪz/
/ʃ/	shop	/ʃɑp/
/ʒ/	measure	/mɛʒər/
/m/	make	/meik/
/n/	nine	/nain/
/ŋ/	sing	/sɪŋ/
/h/	house	/haʊs/
/l/	leg	/lɛg/
/r/	red	/rɛd/
/w/	wet	/wɛt/
/y/	yes	/yɛs/

STRESS

In this book, word stress is shown by underlining the stressed syllable.
For example: <u>wa</u>ter; re<u>sult</u>; disap<u>point</u>ing

LETTERS OF THE ALPHABET

/ei/	/i/	/ɛ/	/ai/	/ou/	/u/	/ɑr/
Aa	Bb	Ff	Ii	Oo	Qq	Rr
Hh	Cc	Ll	Yy		Uu	
Jj	Dd	Mm			Ww	
Kk	Ee	Nn				
	Gg	Ss				
	Pp	Xx				
	Tt					
	Vv					
	Zz					

Tapescripts

1 Identity

🎧 01

Steve
(I = Interviewer; S = Steve)
I: Steve, what would you say was your hometown?
S: Uh…hmm…that's a hard one, because I've traveled around a lot. I guess, uh, Miami. I mean, I lived there for more than twenty years, and that's where I was born.
I: But your parents weren't born there, were they?
S: Oh, no, they were born in Argentina, in Mendoza.
I: And what would they say was their hometown?
S: Well, my Dad's really proud to be Argentinian and proud to be from Mendoza, but he's also proud to be an American—a naturalized American citizen. He's just become American after thirty-five years of living there, and he's really proud of that, but I guess it would be hard for them to answer too.
I: And when someone asks you where you're from, what do you say?
S: The United States. I'm an American—uh, North American.
I: Is that because you live in Panama?
S: Yes, but when I'm back home at my parents' house—they've moved since I moved to Panama—and someone asks me where I'm from, I say Miami.
I: And what would you say was maybe the most important thing for you in defining yourself—you know, your personal identity? Like, is it your city, your country, your language, your job?
S: Well, it isn't my hometown I don't think. Or my country. Maybe it's language, because Miami has two languages, English and Spanish. People there usually define themselves according to their language, so I'd say I'm Hispanic, I guess, or a Latino—Latin—from Miami. But I think it has more to do with my attitude. Yeah, you know, my attitude, my opinions about things, my way of seeing the world, with one foot in Latin America and one foot in the U.S. I guess that's who I am.

David
(I = Interviewer; D = David)
I: If someone asks you where you come from, what do you say?
D: I usually say I'm from North America. Or I guess it depends on who's asking or where I am at the time. Obviously, if I'm back home in Canada, then I give the name of my hometown—Montreal. Even though I haven't lived there in years.
I: Were you born there?
D: Yes, I was—born and raised there. I spent my formative years there, until I was eighteen.
I: And, if you're not in Canada?
D: Well, sometimes when I'm traveling, people assume that I'm American, or maybe they're just using the word American to mean North American. That really bothers me—or not that exactly. It's when I explain that I'm from Canada and they say, "Isn't that American?" Now that bugs me.
I: Is it really that important to you?
D: Oh, that's a big question. Uh, yeah, I guess it is. I suppose it's kind of very central to my identity. It's part of how I see myself, how I define who I am. I speak French, so maybe that's part of the reason that it's so important. I mean, I think the language you speak really defines the way you think sometimes. Or at least I feel like it's another side to me. Like there's my French side, and there's my English side. I haven't lived in Montreal in years, and sometimes I really miss always being with people who switch languages all the time. It's like I'm missing a part of myself.
I: Do you speak French at all now?
D: Yeah, on the phone with the friends I grew up with, or with my brother. Once or twice a week. But that's about all.
I: So, what would you say is your mother tongue, then? French or English?
D: Both, I guess. I mean, I was brought up speaking both as a kid. In Montreal, you're just surrounded by both languages everywhere. On TV, in movies, in school. I guess it's possible to stick to just one language in other parts of Canada. There are people in Quebec who know very little English, just like there are lots of people in western Canada who don't know any French at all.

Valeria
(I = Interviewer; V = Valeria)
I: So if I asked you to say who you are, how you define yourself, what would you say was the most important factor? Your hometown? Your job?
V: Hard to say. Both, I guess. I mean, I've lived here all my life, and so has my family. My family has actually lived in the same house for five generations. Well, O.K. I'm exaggerating a little. But we still have a farm not far away where we go in the summer, and my grandmother was born there and her grandparents before her. I love that house, its big stone fireplaces and high ceilings…
I: So maybe the house is what you identify with?
V: Oh, no, not just the house. The land, the little town nearby, really the whole area.
I: And what about your profession?
V: Hmm, yes, well, being a doctor is kind of the family business. I mean, there again we go back generations…my father, my grandfather…I'm actually the first woman in our family to become a doctor, and I really like the idea that I'm the fourth generation of doctors in the family and that a woman can carry on what was basically a male family tradition until very recently.
I: And did you always know you were going to follow in your father's footsteps? Or did you resist it at all at any time?
V: No, no. There was never any question of resisting at all. I'm really happy with my choice. I truly love medicine. You know, it's such an old tradition, such a—I know this is going to sound a little snooty, like a cliché—but it's such a respected profession, and I feel really proud to be carrying on the family tradition.

🎧 02

a) He's just become an American citizen after thirty-five years of living there, and he's really proud of that…
b) …sometimes, when I'm traveling, people just assume that I'm American, or maybe they're just using the word American to mean North American.
c) I guess it's totally possible to stick to just one language in other parts of Canada.
d) …I've lived here all my life, and so has my family. My family has actually lived in the same house for five generations.
e) …I really like the idea that I'm the fourth generation of doctors in the family and that a woman can carry on what was basically a male family tradition until very recently.

🎧 03

(M = Martha; L = Liz)
M: Oh, you have *Men Are From Mars, Women Are From Venus*. I saw it.
L: Yeah, Trish lent it to me. Have you read it?
M: No, not really. I just saw it in a bookstore and I flipped through it just briefly. I read the first few pages though, the part…oh, what was it? The part about men and women being from different planets. You know. It sounded really funny. I think, uh, it's a nice idea but maybe just a little contrived. Sort of obvious, you know? Have you read it yet?
L: Yeah, I just finished it. I know what you mean about it seeming a little contrived, but I do think it's actually

A77

sort of a neat way of getting the idea across. You know, it's very clear. And it's very original, and I didn't find it at all patronizing.
M: That's good. I got the impression that it's very politically correct. What did you think of it? Do you think that men and women are from different planets?
L: Well, in a way. I actually liked a lot of what it had to say. For example, how men and women cope with stress and problems. How we cope differently. How men like to figure things out on their own.
M: Oh, that's so true.
L: Take time to think things through quietly, all on their own.
M: Well, that really means just bottling things up, doesn't it?
L: Well, it's interesting you say that, because that's exactly what the book predicted that that's how a woman would interpret it.
M: Really?
L: Because women are actually different from men in that they prefer to talk about problems and vent their feelings, whereas, like I said, men think it's more efficient to figure things out on their own.
M: When I was flipping through it, I caught a glimpse, a part about how men really take pride in being able to do things and achieve things without help, totally on their own.
L: I think they do. I think they actually do, and I think that's really the root of some of the problems, because women like to talk things over and express themselves, and it really gets them down if they have a partner who won't tell them anything.
M: Yeah. So what solution did the book come up with?
L: Well, tolerance. You know, the best thing to do is be aware that we're different. Realize that men and women have different styles of approaching things and then learn to put up with it. Makes sense to me.
M: Yeah.

📼 04

My Girl by Madness
My girl's mad at me, I didn't want to see the film tonight,
I found it hard to say, she thought I'd had enough of her.
Why can't she see,
She's lovely to me,
But I like to stay in and watch TV on my own every now and then.

My girl's mad at me, been on the telephone for an hour,
We hardly said a word, I tried and tried, but I could not be heard.
Why can't I explain,
Why do I feel this pain?
'Cos* everything I say she doesn't understand, she doesn't realise,
She takes it all the wrong way.

My girl's mad at me, we argued just the other night,
I thought we'd got it straight, we talked and talked until it was light.
I thought we'd agreed,
I thought we'd talked it out,
Now when I try to speak she says that I don't care,
She says I'm unaware and now she says I'm weak.

📼 05

(B = Brian; S = Suzanne)
B: Hello?
S: Hi, it's me!
B: Hiya! How are you doing?
S: Fine, pretty stressed out, had a hard day at work, you know, the usual.
B: Yeah, me too.
S: So, what about the movie? I just called the theater to check the times, and it's on at 7 o'clock and 9:30. Which do you want to go to?
B: Listen, do you mind if we go another night? I'm tired, I just feel like a quiet night at home—you know, lie on the sofa, watch some stupid show on TV.
S: But it's the last night. You said you really wanted to go!
B: Why don't you go with your sister? You said she wanted to see the movie…
S: This is the third time you've backed out. What's wrong?
B: Nothing. I just don't feel like it tonight, that's all.
S: Come on, if there's something wrong, you can tell me. I'm not going to fly off the handle.
B: There's nothing wrong…
S: Yes, there is. You've been weird for days. You don't talk to me; you don't want to see me.
B: That's not true.
S: Are you bored with me? Is there someone else? Have I done something wrong?
B: No, no, of course not.
S: You never used to shut yourself away like this; you used to want to spend time with me. What's changed?
B: Nothing's changed. Of course I want to see you.
S: But not tonight, right? The football game's more interesting I guess.
B: Oh, you know that's not true. I'm just tired, that's all. It's been a hard day. I just need a quiet night at home…
S: Alone!
B: Look, if it's that important to you, I'll come. What time did you say?
S: No, forget it! I wouldn't want you to go out of your way or anything!
B: Don't be like that. Come on. Should I come and pick you up?
S: No, forget it. I changed my mind. Let's just drop it.
B: Look, I'd love to do something tomorrow, O.K.?
S: Whatever. Suit yourself. You always do!
B: Suzanne, don't… Suzanne. Suzanne?

📼 06

1 But not tonight, right? The football game's more interesting I guess.
2 But not tonight, right? The football game's more interesting I guess.
3 No, forget it! I wouldn't want you to go out of your way or anything.
4 No, forget it! I wouldn't want you to go out of your way or anything!

2 Taste

📼 07

1
Uh, bitter coffee in a plastic cup and milk in plastic containers. Yeah, either that or a greasy burger on a plastic tray. Looks great in the picture but tastes disgusting and is definitely overpriced.

2
Uh…watermelon maybe, or strawberries …no, I know—a big bowl of fresh salad with homemade dressing, served with cheese, bread, and a glass of chilled white wine.

3
Roast dinners, you know, huge slices of roast beef served with mashed potatoes and tiny, sweet green peas, and on top of it all, swimming in it, the best gravy you have ever tasted.

4
Crunchy chocolate-chip cookies dunked in milk while you're curled up on the sofa watching your favorite movie.

5
No food, really—I mean, I associate it more with not being able to eat anything—well, at first, at least…and later…maybe chocolate or fruit for some reason…I don't know, something like strawberries. Yes, sweet ripe strawberries with fresh whipped cream.

6
I don't know—hot chocolate? Uhm, no, some kind of fast food or Chinese takeout—or some kind of microwaveable convenience food that is easy to make.

📼 08

Anne
The food? Mmm, it's delicious, really hot and spicy, but delicate, too. Kind of like a cross between Indian and Chinese food but with its own special flavors. They use a lot of lemongrass and coconut and a lot of fish. I really liked the soups. You can buy them from stalls on the corner of the street. You choose the meat you want in your soup and the kind of noodles—long thin white rice noodles, or big fat, thick yellowish ones, and there are these tubs of spices, too, and you choose as much or as little of whatever you want. Then you sit there on the street, or in the market or wherever you are, and eat it. I had some for breakfast one day—it was great! Really great!

Kim
The food? Well, it took some getting used to. I like hot, spicy food, but this was too much for me at first. I guess I built up a kind of immunity to it as time went by though, and I got to like it eventually. It's nothing like the kind of food we get in restaurants back home. I loved the ritual of it, going to the small street cafés where they serve your food on a banana leaf.

A78 TAPESCRIPTS

They wash the leaf and then serve a huge helping of rice right in the middle and give you generous helpings of all the different sauces. You don't get a knife and a fork. You eat with your right hand, making little balls of rice and then soaking up the sauce with these little balls—it takes a while to get good at it. When you finish, they bundle the banana leaf up with any leftovers and throw it out on the street where the goats and cows eat them. I love that side of it, too—nothing goes to waste!

Bill
The food? Well, to tell you the truth, I didn't really like it that much. It isn't the healthiest of diets. Everything is either fried or cooked in pig's fat, and, mmm, I don't really like cabbage that much, and that's a staple part of their diet, like a lot of places in Central Europe. It's usually pickled and served with sour cream—so, no, it isn't really my favorite. Having said that, there were some things I loved—the bread for example. It's really soft and tasty, and so many different kinds, and the biscuits and pastries are really good too. And some of the soups, the various kinds of goulash—that's their national dish—and the bean soups are really delicious, and the paprika makes them so spicy—great on a cold day.

Steve
The food? It isn't particularly elaborate, but it's good. The seafood is especially good, and there's just such a variety, so many different kinds of shellfish, I wouldn't know the names for half of them in English. Another favorite of mine is the grilled green chili peppers. They serve them up by the plateful so you can share them. There's always one that's so spicy it almost blows your head off. More than anything else, I love the eating-out culture. It's pretty informal; you go to a bar and order huge platefuls of various different specialties and share them, everybody eating off the same plates. It's very sociable—a really nice social eating ritual.

09

a) Mmm, it's delicious, really hot and spicy…
b) Well, it took some getting used to.
c) Well, to tell you the truth, I didn't really like it that much.
d) …and, mmm, I don't really like cabbage that much…
e) …no, it isn't really my favorite.
f) It isn't particularly elaborate, but it's good.

10

(S = Sarah; A = Angela; D = David)
S: …I can't believe he bought her plastic flowers for her birthday. I mean, that is so tacky. That is such bad taste.
A: I don't know. It's the thought that counts.
D: Come on! Plastic flowers don't count!
A: Well, no, it might not be your cup of tea, but you know, one man's wine is another man's poison.
D: Huh?
S: What?
A: Well, I mean, I know people who like plastic flowers, and they don't necessarily have bad taste.
D: It depends what you consider bad taste.
S: Yes, I mean, taste is a very personal thing.
A: Right. Beauty is in the eye of the beholder and that kind of thing.
S: Exactly. Everyone's different, so I guess everyone has a different idea of what good taste is.
D: Right, so it really depends on your own taste, doesn't it?
S: Well, yeah, but having said that, no one thinks plastic flowers are in good taste, do they?
D: No. Good taste is…
A: It's really hard to say what good taste is. Bad taste is like being flashy—you know what I mean, like wearing a big gold medallion or something.
D: Oh yes, definitely! Things like that are awful, aren't they?
A: Socks!
D: Socks with sandals, and white socks with black shoes, definitely!
S: No, not necessarily; some people like them.
A: So good taste is really, I guess, it might be an ability to judge the beauty or the elegance of things.
D: Yes, maybe.
S: No. I don't think beauty has anything to do with it. I think it's knowing what's right for the moment. It's knowing what's appropriate that's good taste.
D: Yes, I think you have a point there. It's also about being able to judge the quality of things. Good quality stuff is usually tasteful. And yes, Sarah, you're right—it's about choosing the right thing at the right time, too.
A: That reminds me of Rebecca the other day at Joann's wedding. Talk about the wrong clothes at the wrong time!
S: What, wearing that blue dress thing?
A: Yeah, it was obviously expensive, but talk about bad taste.
D: Absolutely. She looked completely out of place.
S: Well, yes, I guess you're right. But Rebecca, you know, Rebecca has class, which isn't the same as taste. It's not the same.
D: No, but class doesn't excuse her bad taste.
S: But it does in a way, because having class means being confident in yourself. You don't worry what other people think; you just do what you want to do and people accept you for what you are.
A: But class is about knowing how to behave, not how to dress.
S: I don't totally agree there—not these days. Class means being yourself and not caring what other people think.
D: Sure, but I think there's more to it than that. I think it's that you know how to behave in every circumstance, no matter how difficult the situation might be, and how to deal with it. That's class.
A: Yes, yes, I guess it is. The feeling that you can take everything in stride… you're not fazed by any situation or any group of people, and you just continue being yourself regardless.
D: You're cool; you don't get upset, you don't get uptight, you know? Yeah.

11

(S = Sarah; A = Angela; D = David)

a
S: …I can't believe he bought her plastic flowers for her birthday. I mean, that is so tacky. That is such bad taste.
A: I don't know. It's the thought that counts.
D: Come on! Plastic flowers don't count!

b
S: Yes, I mean, taste is a very personal thing.
A: Right. Beauty is in the eye of the beholder and that kind of thing.
S: Exactly. Everyone's different, so I guess…

c
A: …wearing a big gold medallion or something.
D: Oh yes, definitely! Things like that are awful, aren't they?
A: Socks!
D: Socks with sandals, and white socks with black shoes, definitely!
S: No, not necessarily; some people like them.

d
A: …It's knowing what is appropriate that's good taste.
D: Yes, I think you have a point there. It's also about being able to judge the quality of things. Good quality stuff is usually tasteful. And yes, Sarah, you're right—it's about choosing the right thing at the right time, too.
A: That reminds me of Rebecca the other day at Joann's wedding. Talk about the wrong clothes at the wrong time!
S: What, wearing that blue dress thing?
A: Yeah, it was obviously expensive, but talk about bad taste.
D: Absolutely. She looked completely out of place.
S: Well, yes, I guess you're right. But Rebecca, you know, Rebecca has class…

e
A: But class is about knowing how to behave, not how to dress.
S: I don't totally agree there—not these days. Class means being yourself and not caring what other people think.
D: Sure, but I think there's more to it than that. I think it's that you know how to behave in every circumstance, no matter how difficult the situation might be, and how to deal with it. That's class.
A: Yes, yes, I guess it is. The feeling that you can take everything in stride…

12

1 No
2 Yes
3 Yes
4 Yes
5 No
6 No

📼 13

a) The best way to eat fish is raw.
b) French cuisine is the best in the world.
c) People who smoke in restaurants are inconsiderate.
d) If you want to get to the top, you have to start at the bottom.
e) Life is too short to waste time worrying about what other people think.
f) Travel is the best way of broadening the mind.

3 City

📼 14

(M = Mike; S = Sue)

M: …Thank you, John, and now it's back to the studio for the answers to last week's quiz. Sue?
S: Thanks, Mike. Hello, yes, and there are a few surprises in the answers this week. So let's start with the first question, which I think held the biggest surprise for our contestants. According to data collected by the United Nations, 53% of the world's population lives in cities, while 47% live in rural areas. In the European Union the percentage of people living in urban centers rises to a staggering 74% and an even higher 76% in the United States. It would appear that there is a steady movement toward urban areas and that the proportion of city dwellers will continue to rise. Although it may seem a fairly straightforward question to answer, there is still some discussion as to what the world's largest capital is. This is mainly due to the difficulty in deciding where the world's largest cities actually end, because each of them tends to be surrounded by a mass of satellite towns that merge into one large megalopolis. If we take "city" to mean the population that lives within the city limits, then Mexico City, with a population of more than 20,000,000, is the world's largest capital, followed by Seoul at 12,000,000 and Tokyo at 8,000,000. Likewise, it is difficult to tell what the city with the most traffic in the United States is, mainly because it's difficult to measure accurately. However, it is widely recognized that Los Angeles is the U.S. city that suffers from the worst traffic conditions. It's not known whether this information is based on popular opinion or on statistical data, however. Judging from the entries we've received, this will come as quite a surprise to some of our listeners. On to the fourth question. There is still some debate over this one. The Syrians claim that their capital city, Damascus, is the world's oldest city, though other Middle Eastern inhabitants would claim that their capitals are just as old. Sources seem to suggest that the Syrians are right and that their capital is indeed the oldest in the world, having been continuously inhabited since 5000 b.c. Question five was pretty straightforward. There is no doubt whatsoever about which of the world's capital cities is the highest. La Paz, in the Bolivian Andes, stands two and a half miles above sea level. And finally, the last question, again a fairly straightforward question. The first city to have reached a population of 1,000,000 was Rome, which had a population of over a million during the heyday of the Roman Empire in 133 b.c. London reached the mark in 1810 and New York in 1875. Today there are over 300 cities in the world that boast a population in excess of one million. So, the winners this week are Jane Turbot from White Plains, Carol Jackson from Staten Island…

📼 15

a) It would appear that there is a steady movement toward urban areas…
b) …there is still some discussion as to what the world's largest capital is.
c) …it is widely recognized that Los Angeles is the U.S. city that suffers from the worst traffic conditions.
d) It's not known whether this information is based on popular opinion or on statistical data, however.
e) Sources seem to suggest that the Syrians are right…
f) There is no doubt whatsoever about which of the world's capital cities is the highest.

📼 16

(A = Alison; B = Bart)

A: Have you seen this? The article about that new survey…
B: Yes, I was reading it earlier. No surprises there, I don't think…seems pretty obvious to me. You don't need a survey to tell you that, do you?
A: Yeah, well, I don't know. I mean, it's not that simple, is it? I mean, some people like living in more rural areas.
B: Yeah, and you can see why; less stress, less traffic, less pollution…but I don't think it's just a simple question of what you like, you know?
A: No, it's more like…it seems like it's a question of work and money more than anything else, I guess.
B: Yeah, it said that, didn't it? The main reason was that they couldn't find a job outside the city…
A: Well, it doesn't say that exactly, but yes, it says it's, uh, it's, you know, easier to find work in large cities, and I guess that's true, don't you?
B: Yeah, but I don't think that's the main reason. I mean, it might be the main reason for older people…you know, working people, before retirement age, whatever.
A: Yeah, there's a lot of that.
B: But it seems to be talking more about young people…I mean, the statistics here are referring to people under thirty, and like, even if, even if there were plenty of jobs in the suburban areas, well, they'd still go to the cities, wouldn't they?
A: Do you think so? Maybe you're right. Maybe it's more a kind of lure of the bright lights thing…
B: Yeah, you know, nightlife, music, youth culture in general…
A: Yeah, it says something about that, doesn't it? That part where it talks about, what is it… "spare time activities" or something like that?
B: "Recreational facilities."
A: Yeah, that was it.
B: More like bars and clubs!
A: Yeah, and movie theaters and exhibits and stuff, too.
B: Nah, dance clubs and the chance to meet other young people is more like it.
A: Yeah, O.K., the social side of things, but it's important, isn't it?
B: Yeah, this survey seems to suggest that it's the second most important factor after getting a job. You know, if young people decide to leave their homes in the suburbs, then they believe that the social side of things is the second most important thing they consider. What other things do you think they mentioned?
A: Oh, I don't know. Maybe they said there were more opportunities for continuing their education, like going to colleges and stuff. They might be thinking about facilities for their families in the future, like being near good schools and stuff. Uhm, what about better living conditions…more modern houses that need less work on them and stuff?
B: Yeah, I suppose they're all things you'd have to think about, aren't they?
A: Yeah, the survey really makes a lot of sense.
B: Mmm.

📼 17

(H = Helen; R = Robert)

H: Well, I don't really think it's particularly dangerous. Not any more than any other large city. You have to be sensible, take the normal precautions. I mean, I wouldn't walk down a street and stare at somebody, and I certainly wouldn't walk home alone, and I wouldn't go down unlit alleys, you know, dark alleys at night, and obviously there are certain areas that you just know you wouldn't go into, but I think that overall, it's not a particularly dangerous city.
R: Yeah, I think I agree, but, uhm, actually, there have been a couple of stories in the papers recently about this string of muggings that's been going on.
H: Oh yeah, I read about that. Yeah, because they say things are changing, and things are getting worse in the city. I did have a friend, actually, who was on the subway, and her wallet was snatched from her bag just as the train was coming into the station, and of course the person got off the train right away, and there was absolutely nothing she could do about it.
R: Well, I sympathize with her. I mean, I've seen that happen too, and, uh, you just have to watch it in a place like that, or like the outdoor market.

A80   TAPESCRIPTS

You have to be really careful there because there is a big crowd and a lot of pickpockets, and they can steal something and run away.

H: But I don't think it's really dangerous. They're not violent people; you just have to be sensible and keep your eyes open, and…

R: Well, I don't know. This article I read said that a lot of the thieves were carrying knives, which means if you resist then, uh, you could get badly hurt, so that really makes you think, doesn't it?

H: Mmm, I said it wasn't violent, but maybe it is. I heard about a group of tourists the other day who were mugged. What do you do if you see something like that? You don't really know what's going on, and you don't really want to get involved because you don't want to get hurt.

R: Yes. I think it's stupid to try to be a hero. I mean, you could get very badly hurt, and all they want is just money. I mean, I know that it's a terrible thing to say, but it's just money. It's not worth losing your life over.

H: I guess so. Apparently these guys had a knife, and they cut one of the women's handbags from her shoulder. Actually, I think she thought they were going to stab her husband.

R: Did you hear if anybody was hurt at all?

H: No, no one was hurt. Apparently, the woman had had her passport stolen and her traveler's checks taken, but the sad thing was that they had just arrived and they didn't want to leave all their stuff in the hotel. They thought it was safer with them.

R: Yeah, well, that's a problem with tourists though, isn't it? They're easy targets. They stand out in a crowd. Thieves know they're probably carrying money and documents around, and they don't speak the language, and they're vulnerable, aren't they?

H: Well…

R: I mean, it happens to locals, too. There is a friend of mine who was jumped from behind, you know, and they got her bag and ran away, and she tried to run after them but the thieves were too quick, obviously.

H: Was she hurt at all?

R: No, no, but she was really angry.

H: Of course.

R: She didn't lose anything really valuable, so, uh, she didn't report it to the police.

H: I think she should have done that, actually. I think it's really important when something like that happens, because it might be minor at the time, but it could get worse. I think they really need to know if a crime has happened.

R: Yeah. Well, I mean, there should be more police around anyway, shouldn't there? There should be more police on the streets at night.

H: I think you're right.

R: You can be on main streets and there's nobody, just a police car driving up and down occasionally.

H: I think you would feel better protected.

R: Yeah, and it would keep the muggers and thieves away, wouldn't it?

18

a) …there are certain areas that you just know you wouldn't go into…
b) …actually there have been a couple of stories in the papers recently about this string of muggings that's been going on.
c) …her wallet was snatched from her bag just as the train was coming into the station…
d) You have to be really careful there because there is a big crowd and a lot of pickpockets,…
e) You don't really know what's going on,…
f) …I know that it's a terrible thing to say, but it's just money.
g) Actually, I think she thought they were going to stab her husband.
h) …but the sad thing was that they had just arrived…
i) She didn't lose anything really valuable…
j) I think they really need to know if a crime has happened.

19

An Urban Poem

The most unusual thing I ever stole? A snowman.
Midnight. He looked magnificent; a tall, white mute
beneath the winter moon. I wanted him, a mate
with a mind as cold as the slice of ice
within my own brain. I started with the head.

Better off dead than giving in, not taking
what you want. He weighed a ton; his torso,
frozen stiff, hugged to my chest, a fierce chill
piercing my gut. Part of the thrill was knowing
that children would cry in the morning. Life's tough.

Sometimes I steal things I don't need. I joy-ride cars
to nowhere, break into houses just to have a look.
I'm a mucky ghost, leave a mess, maybe pinch a camera.
I watch my gloved hand twisting the doorknob.
A stranger's bedroom. Mirrors. I sigh like this—*Aah*.

It took some time. Reassembled in the yard,
he didn't look the same. I took a run
and booted him. Again. Again. My breath ripped out
in rags. It seems daft now. Then I was standing
alone amongst lumps of snow, sick of the world.

Boredom. Mostly I'm so bored I could eat myself.
One time, I stole a guitar and thought I might
learn to play. I nicked a bust of Shakespeare once,
flogged it, but the snowman was strangest.
You don't understand a word I'm saying, do you?

4 Talk

20

1

Well, I like to be able to take an active part, so it helps if there aren't some people who hog the conversation all the time, and also people need to have a sense of humor about things, I think, not to take things too seriously, and you need a conversation that flows, so that you can…well, you don't get stuck on one subject.

2

Uhm, a good conversationalist. I'd say it's someone who has a point that they want to get across during the conversation—someone with something to say as opposed to someone who just talks nonstop about various subjects and doesn't focus on one particular subject, and I'd say it was someone who listens to other people as well—uhm, that's what I'd say.

3

When people aren't really interested in what you're saying, uhm, that's so annoying. Also, people who constantly interrupt you with grunts or opinions of their own or whatever, and also some people don't care about whose turn it is to talk, so they just, you know, butt in when you're in the middle of a thought and obviously, you know, when the topic's boring. That's very irritating. And sometimes, you know, the conversation goes nowhere, it's going nowhere, and that is also extremely annoying.

4

I really hate it when I'm with someone who just drones on and on in a conversation and who doesn't give you a chance to speak at all. Oh, and I also really hate it when they just go on and on and they don't care whether you are interested at all in what they're saying. They seem oblivious to how you are reacting to them. I hate that.

5

It's good when you're talking about things that you have in common with the person you are talking to, like you're on the same wavelength, and you can share the same tastes or experiences so you know where the other person's coming from. It's also nice if you can share a joke or a personal story or an anecdote or something like that.

6

I can't stand it when you have to do all the talking yourself, when the other person's not responding, or when they are responding but it's with monosyllabic answers, you know, just going yeah, uh, uhm, and that's all you're getting back, and when you have to work to keep the conversation going, that's really bad, when you're having to hunt around for things to say, because you're just not getting anything back.

21

1

(H = Helen; K = Kate)

H: He can be kind of difficult at times. You know, sometimes he'll just get really angry about something really trivial like, I don't know, not clearing the tables quickly enough or something like that, but he'll rant and rave for a while, and then half an hour later, he'll forget all about it. And then he'll be all sweetness and light after that.

K: The woman I used to work for, she was exactly the same. Do you know, she'd complain about everything, and no matter how clean the tables were, she'd make us clean them over and over again, like three or four times. She'd complain if we were milliseconds late for work, she'd complain if we didn't look good enough, and no matter how late it got she would make us stay until everything had been cleaned.

H: Oh, no, no, he's not that bad. No, he really isn't, and sometimes he can be really nice, really generous. Like sometimes after we close, he'll order in some pizza for everybody, and then we'll all sit around talking and having a bite to eat.

K: Oh, that sounds really nice.

H: Mmm, it is, yeah.

2

(B = Bob; J = Jack)

B: I know, I know exactly what you mean. I mean, sometimes, you know, what I do is, I'll, I'll sit down, you know, I'll get everything ready, and then something catches my eye in the room, like, I mean, I have the TV on, you know, in the corner, you know, I have the sound turned down, but I just notice the picture—and I'm like, well, I have to see what that, I mean I have to see that program, you know, it'll only take twenty minutes, and then of course, then I think of someone I have to call. Oh! It's terrible!

J: I know, just before I start, I'll go and make a cup of coffee, and then I'll just take a break with my cup of coffee rather than work...

B: And you have to make yourself, you know, a peanut butter and jelly sandwich or something to go with it...

J: Absolutely.

B: To go with the coffee. Yeah, yeah, and then you look around and think "Well, I really should clean up a little."

J: Yeah, and you have to wash your coffee cup.

3

(A = Adam; F = Fran; N = Nick)

A: ...Apparently it's doubled in the last two years. It's absolutely mind-boggling.

F: Really? That's amazing. Oh, hang on, hang on. Uh, I'd like you to meet Nick. He...Nick, hi, I'd like you to meet Adam. Adam...Nick.

A: Nick! Nick Watkins! How are you?

N: I don't believe it!

A: We went to school together.

F: No. Really?

N: Gosh! What, twenty years ago?

F: That's a long time.

N: Wow! This is something!

A: Yeah, we used to live next door to each other.

N: That's right. That's right. And you always used to be late to the bus stop.

A: That's right, every morning!

F: I can believe that.

A: Yes, the bus driver would wait for me because he knew I'd always be a minute late.

N: And we would sit at the back of the bus.

A: We would.

N: We had our little club for two.

A: That's right. And you, you'd always forget to do your homework, and you'd have to copy mine.

N: Yes. And do you remember you started me smoking? Remember we'd go down by the river and smoke at lunchtime?

A: I remember, but I stopped smoking a long time ago.

N: Good. So did I.

F: Hey, fellas. Remember me?

22

a) ...he'll rant and rave for a while, and then half an hour later, he'll forget all about it. And then he'll be all sweetness and light after that.

b) ...sometimes after we close, he'll order in some pizza for everybody, and then we'll all sit around talking and having a bite to eat.

c) ...I'll go and make a cup of coffee, and then I'll just take a break with my cup of coffee rather than work...

23

(A = Adam; N = Nick)

A: Yes, the bus driver would wait for me because he knew I'd always be a minute late.

N: And we would sit at the back of the bus.

A: We would.

N: We had our little club for two.

A: That's right. And you, you'd always forget to do your homework, and you'd have to copy mine.

N: Yes. And do you remember you started me smoking? Remember we'd go down by the river and smoke at lunchtime?

24

The children? All grown up and left the nest. Tom, my oldest, got married fifteen years ago to a girl he met outside a fruit stand. Her name's Kate; she was, and still is, a very docile sort of person and was just right for Tom. Tom's very high-strung and always has been. When I think back to his childhood, the picture that always springs to mind is that of him sitting at the piano playing brilliantly and being so involved. But that's what he's like. Whatever he's doing, he'll do it with total commitment and concentration. I guess you could say he's a perfectionist, which must be tiring for Kate sometimes. He's been looking particularly run-down lately, but that's because he works all hours. I tell him it's ruining his health, but will he listen to me? Of course not! Anyway, they have just one child, David. He's twelve now and absolutely wild. Though I don't like to criticize my own son, it's all his fault. He seems indifferent to David's behavior, and though I've heard Kate talk to him about it, he won't listen to her. They really should have been stricter with him from the beginning. They wouldn't listen to me when I told them that a little discipline would go a long way, and now they're paying the price.

My second, Rebecca, got married the same year as Tom and is now in the middle of an extremely bitter divorce. I knew it would end up this way, but there's no use trying to change the minds of two people in love. Fortunately there were no children. Poor Rebecca; she was never very good at making the right decisions, but her eternal optimism will get her through this period, I'm sure.

Now Sam, ahhh Sam, my youngest daughter and without a doubt my favorite, though of course I never let it show. A real rascal when she was young, who would charm everyone. She had us all wrapped around her little finger—a real bundle of joy. A little on the lazy side, but good at heart with a good head on her shoulders. She married Anthony—a real love match, and they're still as much in love now as they were twelve years ago. They have three adorable children—Nicholas, Peter, and Sarah—who are well-mannered and not too noisy.

25

A wealthy woman returned home from a ball. She rang the bell for her butler, and when he appeared, she said, "Edward, take off my shoes," and he did. Then she said, "Edward, take off my coat," and he did. "Take off my dress," and he did. "And now, Edward," she said, "if you want to remain in my employment, you are never to wear any of my clothes again."

5 Luck

26

(M = Mary; S = Sarah; D = Dave; B = Bob)

M: Here are your keys back, thanks. What's that horn on your keyring for?

S: It's a souvenir from Italy. I got it last year when we were there on vacation. It's supposed to bring good luck, but it doesn't seem to be working so far! I guess I did win a few bucks in the lottery a couple of weeks ago, but that's about it!

D: Gullible tourists! It's just a racket to make money! You make your own luck in this world.

S: Oh, yeah? Well, how come people have been carrying around good-luck charms for so long then? I mean, the Egyptians have been carrying scarabs around and wearing them as jewelry for thousands of years. I think the ancient Egyptians believed that the scarabs would protect them from death, and people who died were buried with them.

D: How come you know so much?

S: I'm interested in things like that. Did you know that people in India wear peacock feathers on their clothes to keep evil away?
M: That's interesting, because I heard that peacock feathers are supposed to bring bad luck and you shouldn't have any in your house. The eye pattern on them is supposed to be the evil eye. I remember my brother picking one up once and bringing it home, and my mom wouldn't let him keep it because it was unlucky.
B: Hmm. I've never heard about that, but I know that the eye thing is really popular in Turkey. You see them all over the place there. People hang them in their houses and in their cars, and they're supposed to protect you from the evil eye and bad luck.
S: I've seen them—they're really pretty, aren't they?
D: It's all a load of mumbo jumbo. My girlfriend from college had this little rabbit's foot that went everywhere with her. She kept it on her keychain, but she lost it one day. You should have seen how upset she got! Just a silly little thing like that! What's the point?
S: Well, we all have our own superstitions, don't we? I bet you have a pair of lucky socks or something you wear if you have a special date or an interview or something!
D: I do not!
M: I have a little dragon pin that I wear sometimes. A Chinese friend of mine gave it to me years ago and told me it would protect me against unhappiness and the loss of love. I should have been wearing it the night Phil told me he didn't want to see me anymore!
D: You see? Not a very lucky good-luck charm, is it?
M: I wasn't wearing it though. If I had been, things might have worked out differently.
D: Don't be ridiculous! You believe what you like, but I'm sticking to my theory that life's what you make it, and having lucky rabbits' feet, plastic pigs, or Egyptian beetles isn't going to have the slightest influence on whether I get married, make a million, or get the job of my dreams.
S: You do that!

27

(A = Angela; S = Sarah)
A: Have you read this article about the lottery in People?
S: Yeah, it's fun, isn't it?
A: Yeah. It really gets you thinking.
S: You mean…what you would have done if you had won the lottery? Did you read that article in Living Large about Bertha?
A: Yeah, and all that stuff about what she would have done if she'd actually won "the big one."
S: Yeah, I really like that part about how it would have changed her dog's life, like he'd be wearing a diamond-studded collar right now…
A: Nah, I think it's more likely that she'd be driving a snazzy little red sports car!
S: With her new boyfriend…
A: Yeah, and her gorgeous new clothes.
S: Do you think she would have won the jackpot if she'd been playing her usual numbers?
A: It's possible…
S: I got really close to winning once. If I'd played my brother's birthday instead of mine, I would have won.
A: How much would you have won if you had?
S: Oh, millions probably. I would have bought a new house, a car, and a yacht, and I wouldn't be working as an editorial assistant anymore, I can tell you! I mean, I did win 100 bucks, but I wish I'd chosen 17 instead of 19…I certainly wouldn't be sitting here having this conversation if I had!
A: I never even buy a ticket—it's just a waste of money.
S: Don't be so cynical! If you're not in it, you can't win it!

28

Did I tell you about what happened to us last week? No? Well, we were out at a restaurant, a whole group of us, and of course Kelly had her cell phone with her. Anyway, we were in the bar, waiting for a table, chatting and laughing and having a good time. At one point, Kelly noticed this couple rummaging around in the coats on the coat stand and then getting ready to leave. Well, Kelly was kind of suspicious, so she went over to check if her phone was still in her coat pocket, and of course it wasn't! So she went to follow the couple outside to ask them if they'd taken her phone, and a couple of the others went with her. They were just approaching the couple when Hannah had a brainstorm. She had her cell phone with her, so she called Kelly's number and just as Kelly was asking the couple whether they'd had her phone, it started ringing in one of their pockets! They couldn't very well deny having it and handed it over very sheepishly! Lucky, huh?

29

The way I came to miss the end of the world— well, the end of the world I had known for close on thirty years—was sheer accident: like a lot of survival, when you come to think of it. In the nature of things a good many somebodies are always in hospital, and the law of averages had picked on me to be one of them a week or so before…my eyes and indeed my whole head was wreathed in bandages.

Customarily the west-bound buses thundered along trying to beat the lights at the corner; as often as not a pig-squeal of brakes and a salvo of shots from the silencer would tell that they hadn't.

But this morning was different. Disturbingly because mysteriously different. No wheels rumbled, no buses roared, no sound of a car of any kind, in fact, was to be heard. No brakes, no horns, not even the clopping of the few rare horses that still occasionally passed. Nor, as there should be at such an hour, the composite tramp of work-bound feet.

…"Hey!" I shouted. "I want some breakfast. Room forty-eight!"

For a moment nothing happened. Then came voices all shouting together. It sounded like hundreds of them, and not a word coming through clearly. It was as though I'd put on a record of crowd noises— and an ill-disposed crowd at that. I had a nightmarish flash wondering whether I had been transferred to a mental home while I was sleeping, and that this was not St. Merryn's Hospital at all. Those voices simply didn't sound normal to me. At that moment bed seemed to be the one safe, comforting thing in my whole baffling environment. As if to underline that there came a sound which checked me in the act of pulling up the sheets. From the street below rose a scream, wildly distraught and contagiously terrifying. It came three times, and when it had died away it seemed still to tingle in the air.

You'll find it in the records that on Tuesday, 7 May, the Earth's orbit passed through a cloud of comet debris. All that I actually know of the occasion is that I had to spend the evening in my bed listening to eye-witness accounts of what was constantly claimed to be the most remarkable celestial spectacle on record.

…The nurse who brought me my supper had to tell me all about it.

"The sky's simply full of shooting stars," she said. "All bright green. They make people's faces look frightfully ghastly. Everybody's out watching them, and sometimes it's almost as light as day—only all the wrong colour. Every now and then there's a big one so bright that it hurts to look at it. It's a marvellous sight. They say there's never been any thing like it before. It is such a pity you can't see it, isn't it?"

"It is," I agreed somewhat shortly.
"Oooh!"
"Why 'oooh'?" I inquired.
"That was such a brilliant one then—it made the whole room look green. What a pity you couldn't see it."
"Isn't it. Now do go away, there's a good girl."

Was I more scared of endangering my sight by taking off the bandages, or of staying in the dark?…I had the sense and the self-control to get out of bed and pull the blind down before I started on the safety-pins. Once I had the coverings off, and had found out that I could see in the dimness, I felt a relief that I'd never known before…I discovered a pair of dark glasses thoughtfully put ready…Cautiously I put them on before I went right close to the window.

…At the far end of the wide corridor were the doors of a ward…I opened the door. It was pretty dark in there. The curtains had evidently been drawn after the previous night's display was over—and they were still drawn.
"Sister?" I inquired.
"She ain't 'ere," a man's voice said. "What's more," it went on, "she ain't been 'ere for ruddy hours, neither. Can't you pull them ruddy curtains, mate, and let's 'ave some flippin' light? Don't know what's come over the bloody place this morning."
"Okay," I agreed.
Even if the whole place were disorganized, there didn't seem to be any good reason why the unfortunate patients should have to lie in the dark.

I pulled back the curtains on the nearest window, and let in a shaft of bright sunlight. It was a surgical ward with about twenty patients, all bedridden. Leg injuries mostly, several amputations, by the look of it.
"Stop fooling about with 'em, mate, and pull 'em back," said the same voice.
I turned and looked at the man who spoke. He was a dark, burly fellow with a weather-beaten skin. He was sitting up in bed, facing directly at me—and at the light. His eyes seemed to be gazing into my own, so did his neighbor's, and the next man's… For a few moments I stared back at them. It took that long to register. Then: "I—they—they seem to be stuck," I said. "I'll find someone to see to them." And with that I fled the ward.

…A Triffid is certainly distinctive…a height of seven feet or more, here was a plant that had learned to walk…People were surprised and a little disgusted to learn that the species was carnivorous…but actually alarming was the discovery that the whorl topping a Triffid's stem could lash out as a slender stinging weapon ten feet long, capable of discharging enough poison to kill a man if it struck squarely on his unprotected skin.

6 Mind

30

Mike
Mmm…sight, I guess. Yes, the most important one is sight, I guess…I mean, if you're blind, if you can't see, then although you can lead a full life and all that, I think it does make you more vulnerable, more dependent on other people, I don't know, for silly little things like, for example, like shopping in a supermarket or whatever, and I would really hate it if I couldn't see what things or people looked like…or the expressions on people's faces when they're talking to you. I mean, you wouldn't even know if they were looking at you or whether they looked interested in what you were saying.

Maria
No, I haven't, but I read this article about a man who went deaf, and then his hearing was restored to him, and he spoke about how isolating it can be if you can't hear. He said that you miss out on a lot of things, that although you can communicate fine when you need to, you miss out on the subtleties of a conversation. And the thing he missed most was humor…the humor in spontaneous conversation…because it all gets slowed down when you're signing. And he really missed listening to music; that was the worst part, he said. That and not being able to hear his wife's voice. And he said that it was really strange after he first regained his hearing. Everything sounded much louder. He said he actually misses total silence sometimes, just not hearing anything, and that it can be really relaxing.

Helen
Uhmm, I don't know…but maybe smell, I suppose…like someone can just walk past you on the street, and you catch the smell of their perfume, and it reminds you really strongly of someone…or food…I can't remember where I was the other day, but I suddenly smelled the most wonderful cooking smells; coconut oil and eastern spices, and it reminded me so strongly of my vacation in Thailand…I could see the palm trees, taste the food, feel the sun on my skin…yes, I think smell triggers the strongest, most vivid memories.

Nick
This may seem like a strange answer, but maybe touch…you know, the sense of touch…I think it's probably the one we take the most for granted, being able to feel things, and it's not, it's not, you know, a sense that's limited to one part of your body, either—it's everything, every single pore, every single inch of your skin. I remember seeing a documentary about a man who'd been born deaf and mute and had later lost his sight in an accident—he lived a full life—he was eighty something, and he still worked and even traveled. He just lived his life totally through his sense of touch. In this program they showed him visiting other people like him in Japan. It was amazing. They used an international sign language that was based on touch; they would touch each other and sign on each other's palms, and they could feel each other talking—and it showed them going to a drum concert, too,—like a traditional Japanese drum concert—and they could feel the music, I mean they could feel the vibrations of the drums, even though they couldn't hear them. It was just totally amazing.

Petra
Well, usually I'm renowned for my sense of smell! Sometimes I can smell things that no one else notices. That can be good, because I'm really sensitive to things like gas leaks and anything that smells bad…things like food that's spoiled. My mom often asks me to smell meat or fish or milk or whatever to see if it's O.K.…but, I recently had a bad cold, and it's really affected my sense of smell. I mean, I can smell really strong things, like coffee or if something's burning in the kitchen, but I can't smell other things like perfume, so I don't know how much to put on. And I really miss the subtler smells in the kitchen. It affects my taste, too. Everything tastes so bland.

31

a) Yes, the most important one is sight, I guess…I mean, if you're blind, if you can't see, then although you can lead a full life and all that, I think it does make you more vulnerable, more dependent on other people…
b) …I would really hate it if I couldn't see what things or people looked like…or the expressions on people's faces when they're talking to you. I mean, you wouldn't even know if they were looking at you or whether they looked interested in what you were saying.
c) …I read this article about a man who went deaf, and then his hearing was restored to him, and he spoke about how isolating it can be if you can't hear.
d) …he really missed listening to music; that was the worst part, he said. That and not being able to hear his wife's voice.
e) …I could see the palm trees, taste the food, feel the sun on my skin…
f) …they used an international sign language that was based on touch; they would touch each other and sign on each other's palms, and they could feel each other talking—and it showed them going to a drum concert, too—like a traditional Japanese drum concert—and they could feel the music, I mean they could feel the vibrations of the drums, even though they couldn't hear them.
g) …I'm really sensitive to things like gas leaks and anything that smells bad…
h) …I can smell really strong things, like coffee or if something's burning in the kitchen, but I can't smell other things like perfume, so I don't know how much to put on. And I really miss the subtler smells in the kitchen. It affects my taste, too. Everything tastes so bland.

32

(S = Sue; J = John; P = Pete)
S: Listen, John, would you mind leaving the room for a minute? There's something I need to discuss with Pete.
J: No, of course not. I'm feeling kind of hungry anyway. Would you mind if I ran out for something to eat?
S: No, go ahead.
P: Well, what is it, Sue?
S: I have some bad news.
P: Uh, oh. I think I know what you're going to say. Do you mind if I smoke?
S: Yes, I do mind. You know this is a non-smoking building.
P: Sorry. So what is it?
S: We lost the contract.
P: I guess I'm not that surprised. That's what we get for speaking our minds to the client, right?
S: Yes, I guess so…

33

I'm Going Slightly Mad, by Queen
When the outside temperature rises
And the meaning is oh so clear,
One thousand and one yellow daffodils
Begin to dance in front of you, oh dear.
Are they trying to tell you something?
You're missing that one final screw,
You're simply not in the pink my dear,
To be honest you haven't got a clue.
I'm going slightly mad,
I'm going slightly mad,
It finally happened, happened,
It finally happened, ooh oh,
It finally happened.
I'm slightly mad. (Oh dear!)
I'm one card short of a full deck,
I'm not quite the shilling,
One wave short of a shipwreck,
I'm not my usual top billing,
I'm coming down with a fever,
I'm really out to sea,
This kettle is boiling over
I think I'm a banana tree.